HOW
FLOOR DEALERS CAN
BEAT THE BOXES
ONLINE

THE ONLY 3 ONLINE STRATEGIES
YOU NEED TO ATTRACT UNLIMITED
HIGH-MARGIN CUSTOMERS

The ultimate guide for
simplifying your online marketing,
eliminating tech overwhelm, and
kicking the box stores where it hurts.

JIM AUGUSTUS ARMSTRONG

Flooring Success Systems
236 South 3rd St., Suite 309
Montrose, CO 81401
1-877-887-5791
Support@FlooringSuccessSystems.com

Image Copyright:
Face palm man: durantelallera/Shutterstock
Rattle snake: anton_novik/Shutterstock

Ordering Information:
For information on quantity purchases by corporations, associations, and others, contact the publisher at the address, email or phone number above.

How Floor Dealers Can Beat The Boxes Online: The only 3 online strategies you need to attract unlimited high-margin customers

By Jim Augustus Armstrong. -- 1st ed.
ISBN: 978-1975691349

CONTENTS

Strategy #3:

How to implement all 3 digital strategies in your business

Appendix

ACKNOWLEDGEMENTS

....

Our *Digital Floor Dealer* team: Jen Cisternino, Julie Robertson, and Sheri Bambrough for their dedication to providing outstanding online marketing services for our floor dealer clients, as well as their ongoing input in keeping the program cutting-edge. Tiffany Hoeckelman and the team at Lone Orange for their fantastic design and set up. Linda Senn for her excellent copy editing. Robert Skrob for his ongoing insights and guidance.

And finally, Jolyn Armstrong: my wife, business partner, *Flooring Success Systems* team builder, and my biggest source of inspiration and encouragement. Thank you for all you do to make our business great and our lives phenomenal.

ICONS

....

Case Study

This icon means you're about to read a case study involving a real, live floor dealer using one or more of the strategies taught in this book.

Rule breaker!

This icon means you're about to get tips and strategies that break commonly followed "rules" of the flooring industry. Pay special attention because breaking these rules will help you get an *Unfair Advantage* over competitors, beat the boxes, and dramatically increase your profits!

Watch out!

This icon means you're about to be warned of a deadly pitfall that can hurt your profitability or success.

What the ...?

This icon means that Jim is about to discuss a commonly held flooring industry idea or belief that's so dumb or harmful to dealers that he gets severely torqued off even thinking about it.

JIM'S LEXICON

....

Bottom Feeder. A die-hard price shopper who does not care about quality, craftsmanship, customer service, or great warranties. Is only interested in beating you up on price until your margins are lying on the ground in bloody tatters. If you do land the sale by slashing your prices, God help you. They will reward you by complaining, nit-picking, and making your life hell throughout the entire project. Once you identify a bottom feeder, send them to your competition.

Brand Building. See "traditional advertising."

Bullet-proof, 5-star online reputation. An online reputation of 4-5 stars that's so strong it's unassailable. Even if a competitor or jerk customer leaves fake negative reviews, the dealer's online reputation is so strong that it doesn't affect their business. A bullet-proof reputation is built by implementing the strategies in this book. Dealers who do this create total differentiation from competitors, make themselves the obvious choice to consumers, and magnetically attract the best customers online. They gain an unfair advantage over every other dealer in their market, including box stores. (See *unfair advantage*.)

Direct Response Marketing. The kind of marketing I use and teach. The opposite of "traditional" or "brand building" advertising. It's designed to compel immediate response from your prospects and customers, create total differentiation, and make you the obvious choice. Uses benefits and unique selling propositions instead of product "features." It answers the unspoken question on every consumer's mind: Why should I do business with you instead of your competitor?

Ideal Business, Ideal Lifestyle™. Shorthand for my philosophy that the purpose of your business is to fund and facilitate your *Ideal Lifestyle*. I teach dealers how to build an *Ideal Business* that funds and facilitates their *Ideal Lifestyle*. It's also the name of my newsletter.

Marketing System. A set of interconnected sales and marketing strategies working together to create the Marketing Multiplier effect, create differentiation, reduce price resistance and generate sales. Each strategy in a marketing system compounds the effectiveness of every other strategy. The whole is far more powerful than the sum of its parts.

Name, Rank, And Serial Number Ads And Websites. Ads and websites that follow the following formula:
- Business name at the top
- Photos of products (sometimes with teaser prices)
- Contact information

The majority of flooring advertising follows this formula. The gigantic problem with these kinds of ads and websites is that they create no differentiation from your competitors. And when there's no differentiation, you wind up competing on price.

Offline vs. online reputation. A good offline reputation is what a dealer develops by providing good service, selling quality products, and taking excellent care of their customers.

A dealer's online reputation is what prospective customers see when searching online for flooring. Many dealers have excellent *offline* reputations, but through mistakes or simple neglect have negative *online* reputations. This causes dealers to lose a steady stream of prospective customers without realizing it. (See *online customer leak*.)

Online customer leak. When dealers lose prospective customers because of one or more marketing mistakes made online. After researching online, customers buy from the competition and simply never call or visit the dealer who has online leaks. These leaks are mostly invisible, and the dealer is unaware that they have an ongoing loss of revenue. Most dealers are making one or more mistakes online which cause leaks.

Path-to-purchase. The path consumers take when purchasing big ticket items ($500 or more). Studies have shown that 85% of consumers begin their path-to-purchase online. 70% then visit a brick-and-mortar store. 82% make their purchase in the store. This entire process takes an average of 79 days. The vast majority of dealers have no system in place to continuously stay in front of prospects throughout the path-to-purchase. By implementing the strategies in this book, you will stay in front of prospects throughout the 79 days and capture many of the customers who otherwise would have bought from a competitor.

Purpose Of Your Business. To fund and facilitate your *Ideal Lifestyle*.

Traditional Advertising. Also known as "brand building" or "institutional advertising." It's the opposite of Direct Response Marketing. The basic idea is that you put your business name out there over and over again and hope that if enough people see your name enough times that you'll build up "name recognition," and that this will translate into sales. There's a tiny grain of truth to this. You can generate business this way. However there are three gigantic problems with it: 1) It's very slow; 2) there's a tremendous amount of waste; and 3) it's extremely expensive. Gigantic corporations (like box stores) can afford the time, money, and waste to make this work. Most floor dealers can't. Which is why I teach and use Direct Response Marketing strategies.

Unfair Advantage. This does not mean doing anything illegal or unethical. This means implementing unconventional strategies which (out of ignorance or laziness) most of your competitors won't. It means being willing to use strategies that ignore industry "norms." It describes a maverick attitude that says, "I don't care what everyone else is doing; I don't care what's popular; I don't care what the so-called 'experts' say; I demand big, measurable results from my marketing. Period." This combination of maverick attitude with an industry-defying approach to marketing gives dealers who adopt the strategies in this book a de facto *Unfair Advantage* over all competitors in their market place, including box stores.

Unspoken Question On Every Consumer's Mind. Every flooring consumer has an unspoken question on their mind: *Why should I do business with you instead of your competitors?* The vast majority of flooring advertising and websites do not answer this question, which is why many dealers wind up competing on price.

QUIZ TO DETERMINE IF YOU SHOULD READ THIS BOOK

....

You might be wondering if reading this book is going to be a waste of time—if it will even apply to your business. So I've developed a quiz to help you decide if this is the right book for you. Tell me…

How many of these statements apply to you? Check all that apply.

❑ **"I'm sick of losing customers to competitors."**

❑ **"Online marketing has me totally overwhelmed.** Every online 'expert' tells me I should be doing something different. It seems like there are dozens of things I should be doing online. Who has the time to figure this stuff out?"

❑ **"I feel stuck at the same level in my business.** No matter what I do I can't seem to grow it bigger. I keep hitting my head on a glass ceiling."

❑ **"I paid an online lead company $6,000, and the leads were terrible.** All it generated were price shoppers. Even worse, they would give the same lead to several flooring stores, and I wound up having to slash my margins just to get the sale."

❑ **"For some reason I've gotten negative reviews from people I don't recognize,** probably competitors trying to sabotage my reputation. I don't know how to fix this."

❑ **"I'm not good with technology.** A lot of the stuff I see being done online is over my head. I don't even know where to start."

❑ **"I spent $500 per month for a year on pay-per-click ads and only got a couple of small sales."**

❑ **"A few customers left totally unfair negative reviews.** They made unreasonable demands and then blasted us online when we wouldn't kowtow to them. What can I do about this?"

❑ **"There are 10 different social media platforms** the experts say I have to be using if I want to stand a chance against the boxes and online dealers. How am I supposed to do all that and still run my business?"

❑ **"I want to increase my sales, but most of the advertising I try just seems to be a waste of money."**

❑ **"It seems like the only thing customers care about is cheap price.** I provide great service and products—I really look out for my customers. But it doesn't seem to matter. All they care about is price, price, price. It's discouraging."

❑ **"I have a successful flooring business, and I'm looking for strategies to take it to a whole new level."**

If any of these sound familiar, then you're in the right place. If you feel overwhelmed by all the digital technology and are looking for simple solutions to grow your business, and/or if you're a super successful dealer looking for strategies to make your business even more successful, then this book is for you.

And about the overwhelm...believe me, I get it. You're busy. The flooring business is complex, with many moving parts. It's not like selling coffee tables or lamps, where the customer pays their money and walks out with their product. A flooring sale involves multiple steps, multiple vendors, and multiple people on your team involved with the customer throughout the process: sales, administration, warehouse, installation, etc. With all this going on, who has time to learn dozens of digital marketing strategies? Which is why I want to take a minute pose an important question:

WHAT IF YOU ONLY NEEDED 3 ONLINE STRATEGIES TO BE SUCCESSFUL?

....

What if you didn't have to worry about learning and implementing dozens of strategies? What if instead you only had to focus on three primary things online, and were able to get a steady stream of sales as a result? That's what this book is about— simplifying your life and making your job of getting customers online far easier and much more manageable.

After you read this book, you won't have to worry if you're doing the right things online, because in this book you will discover 3 online strategies to:

- Magnetically attract the best customers who are predisposed to buy from you
- Dramatically increase your sales
- Command margins of 45% - 50% or more (No more competing on price!)

Skeptical? I don't blame you

You may have attended presentations on social media and other digital marketing and not learned anything that helped you get more customers. Or the training may have overwhelmed and confused you more than it helped you. Or, you may have paid a lot of money to companies who promised to get you ranked #1 on Google, or get you a ton of reviews, or lots of likes on Facebook, or whatever they happened to be selling, and the results were lousy. If that describes you, then you are definitely in the right place because out of the 500 ways to promote your business online, I've narrowed it down to three that will give you the biggest results, in the fastest time, for the least money.

And when I say results, I don't mean just "engagement." You hear social media experts saying you need to get prospects to "engage" with you online. They are right: you need engagement, but by itself engagement is useless. Why? Because bankers don't allow deposits of engagements in your bank account. They only allow you to deposit money. And the way you get money is to make sales. So, while engagement is important, it's only the first step.

I'll repeat that: *Online engagement is important, but it's only a first step, and if you don't take it any further your online strategy is INCOMPLETE.*

You've got to turn those engagements into sales. You've got to get people *offline* and *into* your store, and that's what you are going to learn here.

Imagine if you could wave a magic wand...

Imagine you could wave a magic wand and have an online customer-generating machine that sends you an ongoing stream of high-margin customers who are happy to pay your prices even if you're the most expensive, and it runs on autopilot 24/7, even when you're sleeping or on vacation, without all the headaches and hassles, even if you don't know diddly about computers or online marketing.

And imagine if prospects and customers could find you all over the internet, on all the big review sites. Everywhere they looked they'd see you. And you had a stream of 4 and 5-star reviews being posted every week, so you had a bullet-proof reputation online that you could be proud of that made your store the obvious choice, and totally differentiated you from your competitors—and made people eager to buy from you.

How would that make you feel?

Well, that's what I'm going to show you how to do.

Why should you listen to me?

Let me ask you: if you don't do anything differently, how is your flooring business going to look six months from now? Will your competitors be stealing customers from you because they're doing a better job marketing online? Will you be selling on price? Will you be lying awake at night worrying about money? Will you be frustrated because you're not making the money you deserve? Will you be disappointed because you can't provide for your family in the way you want to? Will you be struggling to figure out online marketing, and getting lousy results?

What you're going to learn here will change all of this. So, I encourage you to shut off your phone, close your email, and for the next 60 minutes really pay attention as you read this, because the information I'm going to share with you is an online game changer, and can transform your ability to get the best customers.

My story and why it matters to you

When you're choosing a business mentor it's important that you choose someone who's qualified. Flooring is a unique industry, with unique challenges and opportunities. There are a lot of trainers and marketing companies, that don't know anything about our industry, who are trying to sell you things. There are many people out there who don't know the flooring business, trying to teach business to floor dealers, and that scares me. So, I think it's important that you know a little about me.

I am the *Marketing Mastery* columnist for *Floor Covering News*, I speak at industry trade shows like *Surfaces* and *Coverings*, I produce and co-host the FCNews *Marketing Mastery Webinars*. I'm a member of the *WFCA*. I'm the author of the flooring industry book, *How Floor Dealers Can Beat The Boxes And Escape The Cheap Price Rat Race of Doom Forever*, the predecessor to this book. I founded *Flooring Success Systems* in 2007 because I saw that floor dealers were struggling to compete against the box stores, their margins were being squeezed, and most advertising methods, both print and online, were failing them. I also saw that overwork is epidemic in our industry, with many dealers working 50-70 hours per week or more, feeling stressed out and burned out. I've dedicated my career to helping floor dealers succeed; to make a lot more while working a lot less. (See the Appendix for floor dealer case studies.) So, the most important thing you need to know is that I come from inside the flooring industry. I understand your problems. I understand the big challenges you're facing.

Since launching *Flooring Success Systems* in 2007, over 2,000 dealers have relied on me for marketing advice and strategies to help them grow their businesses while cutting their work hours. I have a private client group with some of the most successful, fastest growing flooring dealerships in the country. Here are just a few out of the many testimonials I have from floor dealers who have transformed their businesses and lives for the better:

"I'm making more and working less!"
"I used to work 'dark to dark,' 70 or more hours per week, including weekends. Now I only work Monday through Thursday. Every week I get a 3-day weekend! My wife and I are building our dream house. Also, my revenue went up by 50% two years in a row, and my margins are at 45%. Your program has changed my life. Thank you!"
—*Craig Bendele, FL*

"I'm Working Less Than 30 Hours Per Week...Business Is Fun Again!" "I spent ten years working nearly 70 hours per week. I was constantly putting out fires while trying to keep my fingers in every pie. I had 'I wish I could find someone like me' syndrome. I was finally getting so burned out that I considered selling my business. Thankfully I discovered Jim Armstrong's program, and began implementing his strategies. In a relatively short time I'd cut my work hours in half. Now I'm working less than 30 hours per week, no weekends. I take vacations whenever I want, and spend lots of time with my family. I increased my revenue by 50% last year. It's hard to describe the feeling of having all that stress gone. I've decided not to sell my business because it's so much fun again."
—*Earl Swalm, Moosejaw, SK*

"Before joining *Flooring Success Systems* my residential margins were below 30%. **Now my margins are at 45% to 50%, and I'm booked solid for 3 months.** I used to be a slave to my store, working 7 days a week, and I'd never taken a vacation. Now I regularly take 4-day weekends and several 1-2 week vacations each year. Since joining I've been able to invest my profits into real estate and I now own 7 rental houses, all but one are paid off. My home is paid off, and my store building and warehouse are paid off. Your program changed my life."
—*Jerome Nowowiejski, TX*

Are you mad yet? Here's why you should be

I hated much of online marketing being pitched to floor dealers, and I put it down and resisted teaching it because it was such an obvious waste of money. I've seen dealers get barraged every day with phone calls, emails and everything else trying to get them to buy website services, SEO, Google local, online directory listings, social media, content marketing, review sites, online leads, pay-per-click, and on and on. Dealers get harassed by all of these internet sales vultures trying to suck them dry with their monthly and annual fees, with zero accountability for generating real, paying customers.

I'm angry because of all the digital "marketing companies" who don't know anything about our industry trying to sell floor dealers shiny objects that don't work. Dealers spend their money and their time doing these online strategies that don't generate sales (or only get mediocre results, or only attract price shoppers) and I'm sick of it. I've been railing against it for a decade.

Remember the old saying that if all you have is a hammer, then everything looks like a nail? Well, that's what it's like with a lot of these companies selling you online marketing services. They happen to sell a lead-generation service, so they make it sound like you've got to buy leads from them or you're going to fail.

I don't work like that. I've dedicated my career to only providing dealers with proven strategies that *actually produce results*. (See the appendix for dealer case studies.)

So I went on a quest to figure out what exactly is the truth and what *isn't* about online marketing. With my access to experts in the flooring industry, and the people that I know at distributors, manufacturers, and associations—not to mention the work I've done with hundreds of dealers—I've been able to identify which online strategies really work for getting customers, and which don't.

And now I am finally revealing the three strategies that generate an ongoing stream of the best customers for flooring dealers online.

8

This book is about simplifying, outlining and breaking down these strategies so any dealer can implement them.

After you read this book you'll be able to ignore the internet vultures and never take their calls again.

Getting lousy results online? Why it's not your fault

If you've gotten lousy or mediocre results from online marketing, it's not your fault. You've likely been misled by "marketing companies" about what works and what doesn't for floor dealers.

Remember: *flooring is unique.* It's totally different than most other products being sold. An online marketing strategy that works for a plumbing company or a roofing company won't necessarily work for floor dealers. But you've got all these companies who don't specialize in flooring trying to sell dealers marketing—marketing that's not geared for flooring. Imagine some website builder who has a brewery, an insurance company and an auto dealer for clients. What the heck does he know about flooring? Zip. Nada. Any dealer who hires this guy is going to get a generic website to try and sell this totally unique product called flooring.

Case in point: when you hire someone to build your website, you're likely to hear him say, "You could do a site like this, or like this, or like this," as he shows you his portfolio of websites he's built for plumbers, florists and coffee shops. That's the problem in a nutshell. You don't need a plumbing website or an e-commerce website that's been reworked for flooring. But that kind of thing happens all the time with dealers, and not just with websites. It happens with social media companies, lead generation companies, print, radio, TV, etc. Marketing companies selling flooring dealers generic, copy-cat advertising.

Proof: How many times have you seen flooring ads or websites that follow this formula:
- Name of the dealership at the top
- Photos of products (sometimes with teaser prices)
- Contact information

I call these name, rank and serial number ads and websites. Browse the internet for flooring dealers, look through your local paper, open your mailbox and this is mostly what you're going to see. Do these ads and websites create any differentiation? No. And when prospects see no differentiation between dealers, how do they make a buying decision?

On price.

But dealers pay a lot of money to put out copy-cat, name, rank and serial number ads and websites designed by these "marketing companies," and then wonder why they get mediocre to lousy results, and why they're attracting price shoppers. (Later on I cover this problem in detail and exactly how to solve it.)

There are dozens (hundreds?) of online strategies that I have seen sold or promoted or promised to flooring dealers—things that may work for a chiropractor or a health club—that are a total waste of time, energy and money for dealers. But that doesn't stop these so-called "marketing companies" from taking your money. And that makes me mad.

It should make you mad, too.

I'm going to help you simplify, simplify, simplify

What you're going to learn in this book are the three online strategies out of the hundreds that you should focus on. Yes, there are other digital strategies besides those outlined in this book that can generate a few bucks for your business. But I want to help you *simplify, simplify, simplify*. My goal is not to overwhelm you with every possible online strategy that might possibly generate a sale. You've likely attended digital marketing seminars or webinars that gave you dozens of ideas to do online. Most of these trainers are highly knowledgeable, and they work hard to provide good value by giving you tons of information. The problem isn't the information or the trainers. The problem is that dealers leave with binders full of notes which often wind up collecting dust on a shelf. Not much changes in their business because all that good stuff they heard was too overwhelming to implement because they're so busy.

Look, you don't need tons of information. You don't need dozens of strategies you should be doing online. You're overwhelmed enough as it is.

So, we're going to focus on three—and *only* three—proven strategies that can give you the biggest results (sales), in the shortest time, for the least money. And beyond that you can get on with your life, and run your business, and go fishing, or go golfing, or spend time with your family, or whatever else you want to do. You no longer have to worry about all those calls you're getting from people from outside our industry trying to sell you marketing that's not geared for your unique needs as a flooring dealer. You don't have to feel stressed out or guilty because you're not implementing the ten-dozen online marketing tactics you heard in a seminar, webinar or article.

My promise to you

My promise to you is this: I'm going to give you 110%. No hype. No B.S. No overwhelming you with 500 things you "should" be doing online. I am going to cut through the digital jungle and bring you three strategies that will magnetically attract the best customers and give you a huge advantage over boxes and other competitors. If you hang with me and read this short book cover-to-cover you'll know what it takes to win big online.

How would it feel to have an online marketing system in place that magnetically attracts the best customers who don't shop you and are happy to pay margins of 45% or more? How would it feel to have this in place within the next 29 days?

It can happen, but you must commit to taking action. You can't just read this book and then put it on a shelf to collect dust without doing anything. A handful of dealers are going to take what they learn in this book, take action, and crush it. They are going to get an enormous competitive advantage over their competitors, and digitally dominate their market.

I hope that you're one of those dealers.

STRATEGY #1:

....

GENERATE BIG PROFITS BY CREATING A BULLETPROOF, 5-STAR ONLINE REPUTATION

FLOOR DEALER: We've been in business for 50 years and we have a great reputation.

JIM: That's good, but I noticed that you've only got 6 online reviews, and your average rating is only 2.1 stars. If you were searching online for a flooring store, would you choose one with a 2-star rating?

FLOOR DEALER: Uh…

4 reasons why positive reviews mean big profits for your business

Here's a question I ask dealers attending my webinars and live trainings: *are new customers more distrustful and skeptical than they were 10-15 years ago?* The overwhelming answer is always "yes."

Why the growing distrust...? It's because your prospective customers have been lied to and ripped off by flooring companies, or they know someone who has. They've also been lied to and ripped off by politicians. By Wall Street. By internet scams. They've been "spied on" by their own government. The financial meltdown and collapse of the housing market in 2008 has left a permanent mindset of caution and fear in their minds. Is it any wonder new customers who haven't bought from you before don't trust you? Why should they? As far as they know you could easily be another company out to lie to them and rip them off.

Reason #1: Reviews quickly build trust

Reviews help you quickly establish trust in a distrusting world. Research backs this up. According to BrightLocal, 88% of consumers trust reviews as much as personal recommendations. Think about that for a minute.

> 88% of consumers trust reviews as much as personal recommendations.
>
> -BRIGHTLOCAL

If you're like most dealers, referrals are a huge source of revenue for you. Since most of your potential customers trust reviews as much as a referral, you cannot afford to ignore online reviews.

Reason #2: 90% of consumers read online reviews before visiting a local businesses

I read reviews constantly. Whenever I go to a new restaurant or hotel, or use any local business I check their reviews. I'll bet you do the same at least some of the time. Well, according to *Business 2 Community*, **90% of consumers read online reviews before visiting local businesses.** Your prospects and customers are doing the same thing with your business. Don't kid yourself that they are not. If you don't have reviews, or if your average rating is low, or if all your reviews are more than a few months old, you're losing customers to the boxes. You've got an invisible online customer leak.

Reason #3: 92% of consumers would use a business with a 4-star rating (Business 2 Community)

Consider this: if you generate a 4-star average rating online, over 90% of consumers who are looking for flooring would use your store. Think about the online marketing advantage you would have over competitors, including box stores, by doing this. Conversely, think about the advantage a competitor would have over *you* if they get a 4-star rating and you don't.

> Star rating is the average number of stars you have on a review site. For example, if you've got 20 reviews on *Google My Business*, Google displays the average star rating of those 20 reviews.

Reason #4: Old reviews are not relevant

According to BrightLocal, **73% of consumers think that reviews older than three months are no longer relevant.** It's not enough to get a handful of good reviews, set it and forget it. You've got to have a system in place that generates ongoing reviews.

In summary, by having an ongoing stream of positive reviews, you build instant trust with prospects, you make your business the obvious choice, and you create an enormous advantage over competitors.

Case Studies: 3 dealers who are getting clobbered online

Let's take a look at some examples of real dealers and their online reputations. I found these dealers by Googling a random, average sized city and the word "flooring." (e.g. Cincinnati Flooring.) I've blocked out the names and contact information because I don't want to embarrass anyone, but these are real dealers. I'll call the city "Random City," and refer to the dealers as Dealer 1, Dealer 2 and Dealer 3.

In figure 1.1 are the top three dealers in the organic search using the keywords "Random City Flooring." We'll analyze them one at a time.

Figure 1.1

Dealer 1

In Figure 1.2 you'll see that Dealer 1 has a 5-star average rating. This seems great on the surface, but let's dig deeper. In figure 1.3 you'll see that we've clicked on the listing and opened up the details so we can see the reviews themselves.

16

Figure 1.2

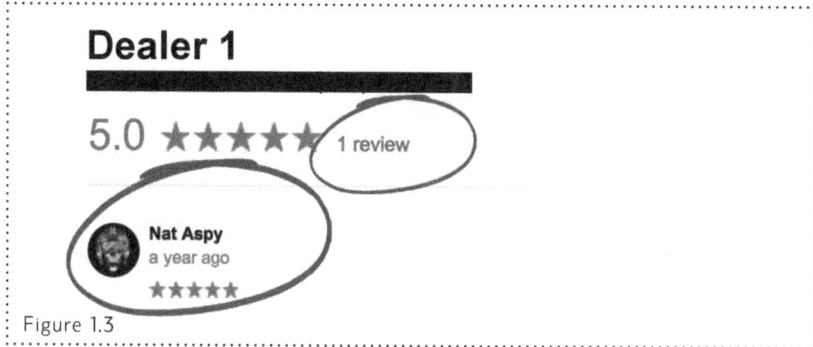

Figure 1.3

Why Dealer 1 is vulnerable

- He has a 5-star rating, but he's only got one review. All it takes is for him to get a couple of 1-star ratings from a competitor or jerk customer, and his average will drop to 2.3.

- The one reviewer didn't even leave a comment.

- The review is a year old. Remember: 73% of consumers consider anything older than 3 months to be irrelevant.

- He's created no differentiation from competitors, so he winds up attracting "price shoppers" and having to compete on price.

  He's done a poor job of positioning himself as an expert Trusted Advisor online, so when prospects visit his store they have a preconception that there is nothing special about his store and that there is no real reason to trust him or buy from him over anyone else. All this simply because his online reputation is not good.

✘ Online reputation grade: D-

He may be hard-working, providing great service for his customers, and his customers might love him. He may have a stellar OFFLINE reputation, but he hasn't turned that into a good ONLINE reputation, so he winds up with a D- in spite of all those great things about his company. This may not be fair, but that's the reality. If you ignore that reality of the importance of having a strong, bullet-proof online reputation, your business will suffer no matter how good you are.

Dealer 2

In figure 1.4 I've clicked on the listing for Dealer 2 so you can see the reviews. He has an average rating of 5-stars, but he has many of the same problems as Dealer 1.

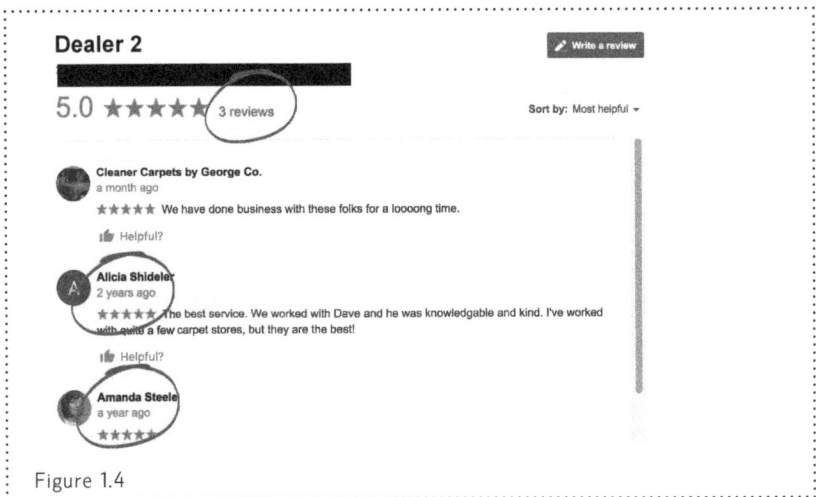

Figure 1.4

Why Dealer 2 is vulnerable

• Only 3 reviews. A couple of negative reviews from a competitor or jerk customer will knock his average rating way down.

• Two of the reviews are a year or more old. 73% of consumers consider these reviews irrelevant.

- No differentiation from competitors, so he winds up attracting "price shoppers" and having to compete on price.
- He's done a poor job of positioning himself as an expert Trusted Advisor, so when prospects visit his store they have a preconception that there is nothing special about his store and that there is no real reason to trust him or buy from him over anyone else, all because his online reputation is not good.

✖ **Online reputation grade: C-**

Dealer 3

In Figure 1.5 you'll see that Dealer 3 has a 2.6-star average rating. Not good, but as we dig deeper you'll see that the problem is even worse.

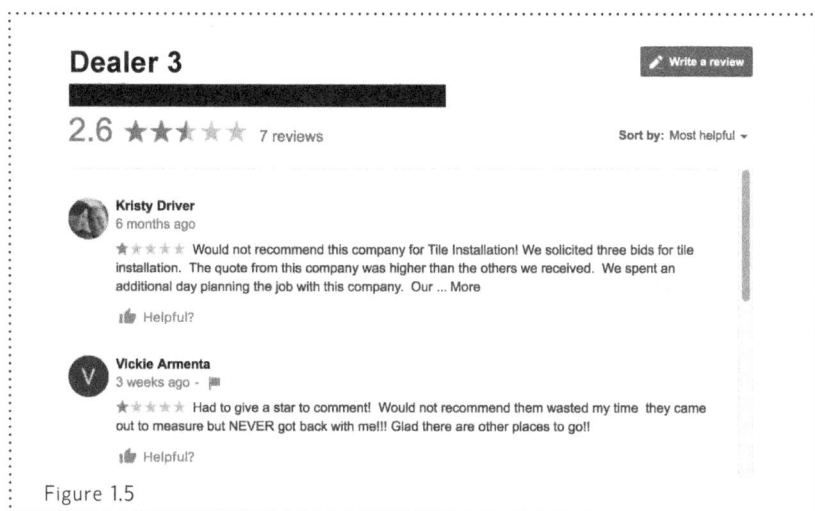

Dealer 3

🖋 Write a review

2.6 ★★★★★ 7 reviews

Sort by: Most helpful ▾

Kristy Driver
6 months ago

★★★★★ Would not recommend this company for Tile Installation! We solicited three bids for tile installation. The quote from this company was higher than the others we received. We spent an additional day planning the job with this company. Our ... More

👍 Helpful?

Vickie Armenta
3 weeks ago - 🏳

★★★★★ Had to give a star to comment! Would not recommend them wasted my time they came out to measure but NEVER got back with me!!! Glad there are other places to go!!

👍 Helpful?

Figure 1.5

Dealer 3

█████████████████████

2.6 ★★★☆☆ 7 reviews

Write a review

Sort by: Most helpful ▾

Sarah Davis
4 months ago

★☆☆☆☆ Beware, this company does not do what it promises and then overcharges. I got three quotes for carpet cleaning and this company was one of the highest ones so I figured they might do a great job but NOPE. My carpets were still stained and wet for 12 hours. Would not use again ever!!!

👍 Helpful?

Response from the owner 3 months ago
We have not cleaned for a Sarah Davies since July 2013. Not sure why it has taken so long to respond. We would like to talk to Sarah. If she would call the store we would like to know why. Thanks Good Shepherd Flooring

D See
11 months ago

★★★★★ I have used this company for years. From cleaning my carpet to now installing my hard wood flooring this weekend. They have always treated me with respect, kindness, and gave me great pricing. ... More

👍 Helpful?

Steve Goodknight
9 months ago

★★★★★ Great service and people, Chris worked with me on a project and was always super professional and did everything he said he would do, lots of options in the valley, these guys are the best.

👍 Helpful?

Arthur Decko
3 years ago

★★★★☆ I went in to get a floor installed, the job turned out to be bigger than expected, and not as simple as it should have been. They worked with me and got it done. Super professional, excellent product, excellent service. I would recommend them based off my experience.

👍 Helpful?

Becca Sroufe
5 months ago - ⚑
★☆☆☆☆

Response from the owner 5 months ago
We are not able to find where we have ever done business with this person. Would like to have more clarification of the problem so we could deal personally with what ever grievance this person may have. Good Shepherd Flooring Center

Figure 1.5

Why Dealer 3 is vulnerable

- His average review rating is 2.6. Very bad.

- The 3 good reviews are 11 months or older. 73% of consumers consider these irrelevant because they're over 3 months old.

- There is an excellent chance he's been sabotaged by fake reviews from competitors, a disgruntled employee, or a jerk customer. (I'll talk about how to solve the "fake review" problem in a minute.)

- There's no differentiation from competitors, so he winds up attracting "price shoppers" and having to compete on price.

- He's totally failed to position himself as a Trusted Advisor online. When prospects visit his store they have a preconception that there is nothing special about his store and that there is no real reason to trust him or buy from him over anyone else, all because his online reputation is not good.

✘ **Online reputation grade: F**

Dealer 3 is getting clobbered and doesn't even know it

Here's Dealer 3 getting up every day trying to build his business and he's getting his head handed to him on a stick by the boxes because he's got hardly any reviews, and half of them are bad.

Imagine you're an average consumer living in "Random City." You don't know anything about flooring, and you're trying to decide on a flooring dealer—a dealer where you're going to invest $8,000 to buy floors for your home. So, you do an online search for "Random City Flooring," and after reading the reviews you figure you have two options:

Option A) use a guy like Dealer 3 with lousy reviews.

Option B) go with a big company like Home Depot. You've grown up with them, you're familiar with them, you see them constantly on TV and hear them constantly on the radio. Not to mention that you've been there 10-15 times a year for the last 10 years to buy tools and garden supplies. It's familiar. It's comfortable.

Which one are you going to choose?

Here is Dealer 3 who's trying to put food on the table and he doesn't even know that he's got this online customer leak. He goes out and measures homes, and puts together estimates, spending hours and hours of his time. And he can't figure out why he's only closing 3 out of 10 prospects. He's been in business 20 years, he takes care of his customers, he honors his warranties. He's got a great OFFLINE reputation that he's spent years working hard to build. But his close ratio is lousy, and he's constantly having to compete on price. He's totally baffled, frustrated and discouraged. He's working in the "estimate" business instead of in the flooring business.

Why is this happening?

Because he doesn't realize that within 30 seconds of leaving the house, Mrs. Prospect picks up her smartphone and within 3 clicks finds him online, sees his 2.6-star rating, and BOOM... he's off the list. (Or, he never gets called to do an estimate in the first place.) And everything he's done up to this point—all the work, all the hours invested, all the advertising money spent—it's all for nothing because he doesn't have this simple thing taken care of: *his ONLINE reputation*.

And it's totally unnecessary.

How an Iowa dealer brought his store back from the brink of disaster

Matt Capell bought Capell Flooring & Interiors in 2008. At that time the business grossed $2 Million, but the margins averaged 20%. Like many dealers, the recession hit Matt very hard, and in 2010 he only grossed $400,000. (This was due in part to all the contractors filing bankruptcy and stiffing him on what they owed.)

This was an incredibly stressful and scary time for Matt and his wife. In fact, things got so bad that they considered closing the business.

So he made a decision. Matt begin looking for the cheapest ways to market his business in an attempt to turn things around.

His store location is not highly visible because it's not on a major road or highway. He tracked where his customers were coming from and found that he got them in three primary ways: 1) Repeat customer, 2) referral, and 3) online. In fact, most of his new customers find him online.

So, Matt began dialing in his online review system, using the strategies contained in this book. As a result he brought his business back from the brink, and is making more money than ever before. Check out what Matt said about his turnaround:

"The recession hit hard. By 2010 our revenue was down to $400,000, and my wife and I were considering closing the doors. I began using the online strategies Jim teaches, and it literally saved my business. Last year we did $2 Million at 40% margins." *-Matt Capell*, ID

23

In figure 1.6 you can see how he made this happen. He has over 120 reviews with an average 5-star rating. Google loves reviews, so Matt almost always comes up in the top three of organic search results. He absolutely blows away the other two stores in the top three, one of which has no reviews and the other is sitting at a 2.7 star rating.

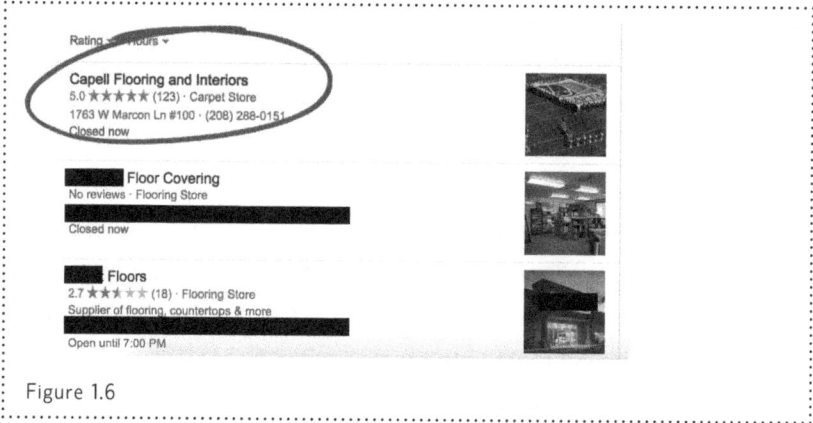

Figure 1.6

In figure 1.7 I've clicked on the listing so you can see the reviews themselves, and why Matt's online reputation is totally bullet-proof.

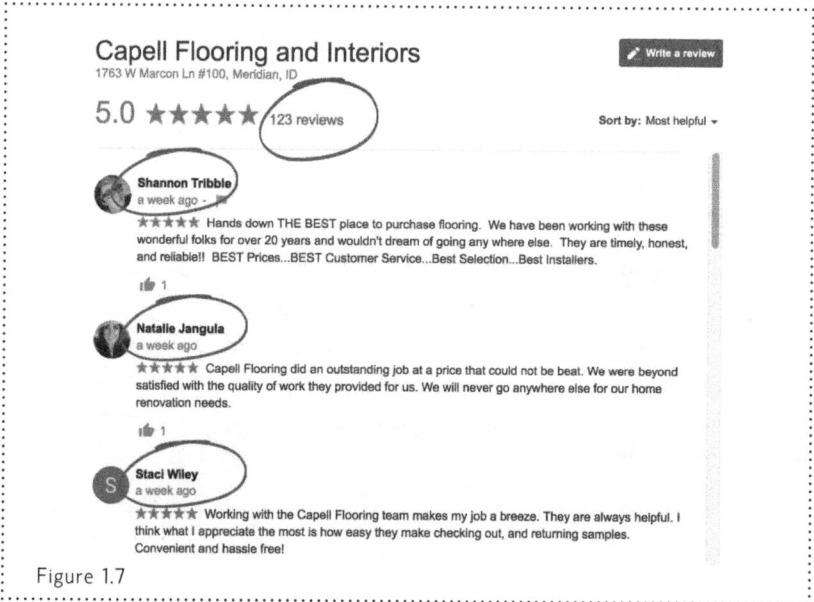

Figure 1.7

Why Capell Flooring is bullet-proof

- He has over 120 reviews. If a competitor, disgruntled employee or jerk customer leaves a fake 1-star review, it won't hurt him. The best way to neutralize poor reviews is to overwhelm them with 4-and-5-star reviews. This brings your average rating up. Also, the negative comments won't hurt you as long as the majority of the comments are positive. Matt's position is unassailable.

- The reviews are recent—within the past week he's gotten three positive reviews. Reviews need to be recent in order for consumers to consider them relevant.

- With a high rating, Matt only attracts customers who want the best. It helps filter out price shoppers.

- He's differentiated himself so strongly that he's in a category
  all by himself. He's made the competition irrelevant.

- Matt has made his store the obvious choice.

- He's overwhelmingly positioned himself as THE Trusted Advisor in his market.

✓ **Online reputation grade: A+**

When a customer walks into his store, she has already been *wow'ed*. She's seen over one-hundred 5-star reviews. She views him as *the* expert, *the* Trusted Advisor in her town. She's not expecting him to be the cheapest.

Let me repeat that because it's important: **she's _not_ expecting him to be the cheapest, yet she still visits his store.**

When he quotes her a price higher than his competitors, in the back of her mind she's thinking, "Over 100 other people paid his prices, and were so thrilled with his service they took the time to go online and give him a 5-star review. He must be worth it." His price is totally justified in her mind.

In fact, here's what Matt said about commanding premium prices:
"My customers regularly tell me I'm way higher than other estimates, and they still buy from me. I just bid a $60,000 job, and the next highest bidder was $8,000 lower. I got the job. My online reviews are big part of why I'm able to sell at prices higher than my competitors."

Why the deck is stacked unfairly against you

One of the things I've discovered in my analysis of flooring dealers is that they're extremely vulnerable if they haven't bullet-proofed their online reputation. When you're going up against the big box stores, they've already got that big name behind them— Home Depot, Lowes, RC Willey, Lumber Liquidators. They have massive advertising budgets and can afford to saturate the airwaves. Their names are all over TV, radio, the internet, display ads, and direct mail. Consumers have heard these names over and over again from the time they were kids—for decades in some cases.

On the other hand, you don't have a name that consumers have heard throughout their lifetime. You don't have that built-in confidence and familiarity that these massive corporations do. It can seem hopeless.

How you can win the battle against the boxes

But you can develop advantages that the big boys don't have, and a big one is to build a bullet-proof 4 to 5-star reputation. It's essential today that you have lots and lots of positive reviews so prospects trust you and believe that you're a legitimate dealer, and that you're going to deliver on your promises. Your prospects go to reviews in order to make sure that you're the type of person that delivers. If you don't have a lot of reviews there, or your rating is low, or you don't have any recent reviews, then you're losing business to the big boxes because they have a brand name that people trust. You've got on online customer leak.

You don't have the multi-million-dollar budget to sponsor a NASCAR team and have your name go around the track every weekend on a racecar; or to pay $3 Million dollars for a 1-minute Super Bowl commercial. Because of that you've got to have reviews.

This dealer is kicking the box stores where it hurts

Check out the reviews from the big boys in Matt's area (fig. 1.8):

MATT IS KICKING THE BOX STORES' WHERE IT HURTS...

Lowe's Home Improvement
3.5 ★★★★★ (43) $ - Home Improvement
Home-improvement chain for appliances, gardening
supplies, tools & more (some offer truck rentals).

RC Willey
3.2 ★★★★★ (127) Furniture Store
Retailer of home furniture, electronics, appliances,
mattresses and flooring

Lumber Liquidators, Inc.
3.5 ★★★★★ (3)
Lumber Liquidators is the nation's largest specialty
retailer of hardwood flooring. Shop laminate flooring,
handscraped and engineered hardwood, bamboo ...

Empire Today
3.5 ★★★★★ (2)
Empire Today® Makes Beautiful New Carpet And
Flooring Easy. 1. Schedule Appointment. Schedule
a FREE In-Home Estimate.

The Home Depot
4.0 ★★★★★ (43)
The Home Depot, Inc. or Home Depot is an
American home improvement supplies retailing
company that sells tools, construction products...

Figure 1.8

27

Most of these companies' online reputations don't hold a candle to Matt's, both in number of reviews or their average rating. The exception is Home Depot, which is actually doing pretty well with their reviews, but Matt is still beating them. Also, when someone clicks on Home Depot's listing, they'll see that most of the reviews are for hardware, tools, and other things besides flooring.

So, don't think box stores will automatically get low ratings. They might not, which makes it even more important for you to have a ton of great reviews. Getting lots of online reviews doesn't just level the playing field, it tips it in your favor. Plus, you don't have to spend a fortune on it.

CASE STUDY

Matt's massive market advantage

The recession knocked Matt Capell's revenue down to $400,000, and he and his wife were considering closing their doors. He quickly turned things around by utilizing the strategies you're learning in this book. Here's a summary of what he accomplished:
- His annual sales are back up to $2 Million and climbing
- His margins are at 40% (up from 20%)
- He credits the reviews and local online marketing for literally saving his business.
- Every day new customers tell him they found him online
- His Customers regularly tell him that he's the highest priced, but they're buying from him anyway. Case in point: Matt bid on a flooring & remodel job and was at $60k, and the customer told him the other bid was $52k. He was $8,000 higher and still got the job.

Five steps to a bullet-proof, 5-star online reputation

Step 1: Claim your listings on all the major review sites

This means making sure your business is visible on all the review sites where your business can and should be listed—where consumers local to your market are. Here's a partial list:

- Google My Business
- Facebook
- Yelp
- Angie's List
- Houzz
- Home Advisor

Make sure you set up each profile correctly. This is very important, because if you don't set each one up right it can hurt your visibility. One common mistake dealers make is having inconsistent information in their profiles: different phone numbers, different street spellings, etc. The Google search-bots don't like this, and it can hurt your visibility online. Make sure you use the same phone number on each profile. If your address has the word "street" in it, spell it "street" across all your profiles. (Don't spell it "Street" on one profile and "St." on another.)

Watch Out!

Are you invisible online?

Many independent dealers don't have the right kind of visibility online. Home Depot, Lowes, Empire, and Lumber Liquidators are highly visible online, and to make matters worse, they have top of mind awareness because they spend a fortune on TV, Radio, print ads, direct mail—you name it.

You have an uphill fight, because when a consumer goes online to look for flooring, the names *Home Depot, Lowes, Empire* and other gigantic companies are already etched in their mind. If your prospects and customers can't quickly find you when they go online, you'll lose them to the boxes, and companies they CAN find online, which includes not only the boxes, but any local competitors who are doing a better job than you at this.

Figure 1.9 illustrates how we set up the next four steps for our dealers: review request, filter, acquisition and amplification. Let's break down how we do it so you can model it in your own business.

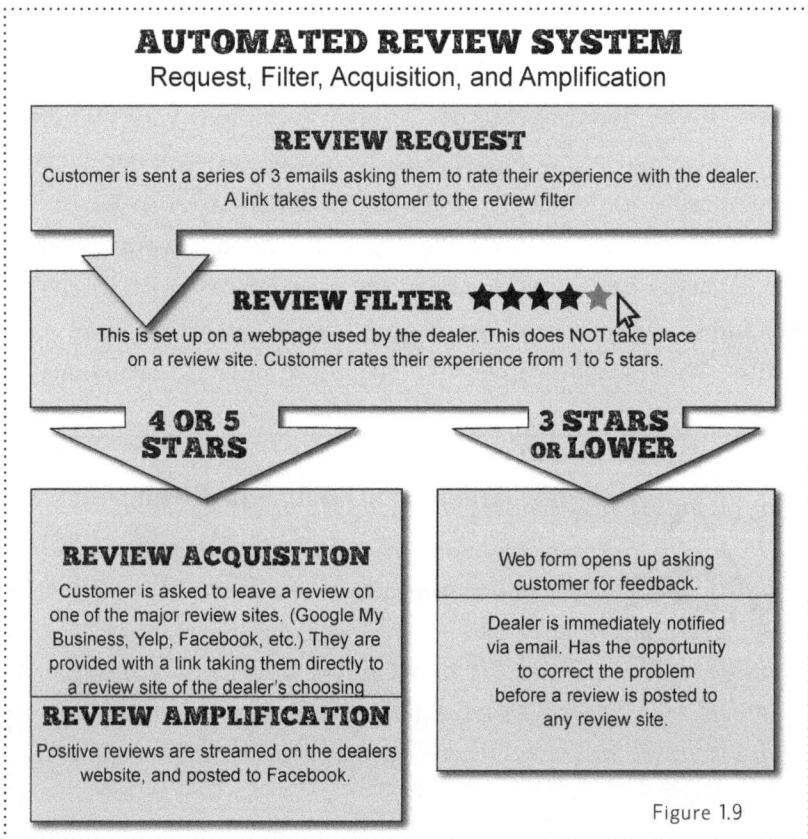

AUTOMATED REVIEW SYSTEM
Request, Filter, Acquisition, and Amplification

REVIEW REQUEST
Customer is sent a series of 3 emails asking them to rate their experience with the dealer. A link takes the customer to the review filter

REVIEW FILTER ★★★★★
This is set up on a webpage used by the dealer. This does NOT take place on a review site. Customer rates their experience from 1 to 5 stars.

4 OR 5 STARS

3 STARS OR LOWER

REVIEW ACQUISITION
Customer is asked to leave a review on one of the major review sites. (Google My Business, Yelp, Facebook, etc.) They are provided with a link taking them directly to a review site of the dealer's choosing

REVIEW AMPLIFICATION
Positive reviews are streamed on the dealers website, and posted to Facebook.

Web form opens up asking customer for feedback.

Dealer is immediately notified via email. Has the opportunity to correct the problem before a review is posted to any review site.

Figure 1.9

Step 2: Review request

There are multiple ways to request reviews. One of the highly effective methods we implement for dealers is a 3-step email campaign. After the installation, each customer gets a series of three emails which go out on day 1, day 3 and day 7. Each email contains a link taking them to the review filter. Once they respond they are taken off the campaign so they don't continue getting emails. (Sending review requests via email is how Matt got most of his reviews.)

Step 3: Review filtering

The customer clicks the link in the review request email. They are taken to a web page used by the dealer, and have the opportunity to rate their experience from 1 to 5 stars. This does NOT take place on a review site. This is important because you might get a customer who is unhappy with your service. Even the best dealers get the occasional disgruntled customer. The last thing you want to do is send unhappy customers to the review sites until you've had a chance to correct the problem.

If the customer gives a rating of 3 stars or lower, an online form opens up where they can leave feedback on what caused them to be less than 100% satisfied. The dealer is notified immediately via email of negative ratings so steps can be taken to correct the problem and turn an unsatisfied customer into a raving fan. By doing this you can transform a lot of negative ratings into 4 or 5 stars.

Competitors, disgruntled employees, or jerk customers can still go directly to the review sites and leave fake negative reviews. This problem is solved with step 4.

Step 4: Review Acquisition

When a customer gives one of our dealers a 4 or 5-star rating in the review filter, the customer sees a message inviting them to leave a review on one of the major review sites such as Google My Business, Facebook, Houzz, Yelp, etc.

A link in the message takes the customer directly to the review site of the dealer's choosing. I recommend driving customers to the sites where you are most in need of reviews. If you don't have any reviews at all, start with Google My Business.

Step 5: Review Amplification

The 4 and 5-star reviews are streamed on our dealers' websites as they are posted. Every time a prospect visits the dealer's site, they are seeing an ongoing stream of new, positive reviews from all over the internet. These reviews are also posted on the dealers Facebook page.

Google likes reviews. By setting up review acquisition and amplification as I've described, it will help your Search Engine Optimization, and help you to appear at the top of the organic search, just like happened with Matt. It's going to help the best customers find you.

Getting lots of positive reviews also protects you against fake negative reviews left by competitors or jerk customers. Let's say on Google My Business you've got fifty 4 and 5-star reviews, giving you an average rating of 4.5 stars. It won't matter if you get a few 1-star reviews. Your average star rating will experience little to no change. Also, consumers realize that even the best companies get negative comments occasionally. As long as you've got lots of positive comments and a high average rating, a few negative comments won't hurt you.

Watch Out!

The importance of automation

I urge you to not try and do this manually—it's too much work, and time is better spent on other aspects of building your business. We ALWAYS automate this when we set it up for dealers so it runs 24/7, even when they're on vacation or sleeping. Otherwise the steps won't get done, or it will be inconsistent.

Remember: 73% of consumers think that any review older than three months is irrelevant. This means you've got to have an ongoing stream of positive reviews, and automation insures this will happen.

Don't bombard the internet with reviews

If the Google-bots see a whole bunch of reviews suddenly appear on your review sites they get suspicious and your visibility can be hurt. It's important that you get a steady stream of reviews that are dripped out consistently. Automation can make this happen in a way that the Google-bots like to see.

Later I'll tell you how you can get this set up so it's totally automated.

JIM AUGUSTUS ARMSTRONG

STRATEGY #2:

....

THE FACEBOOK CUSTOMER-GENERATION SYSTEM

FLOOR DEALER: I keep hearing about all the different social media platforms where I should be marketing my business. But there are so many. I just can't keep up.

JIM: How about focusing on the *one* platform where most of your customers are?

Why Facebook?

There are many social media sites, but only a few can generate enough customers to be worth bothering with. My goal with this book is not to bombard you with every social media platform and online strategy that could possibly generate a few bucks. My goal for you is *simplify, simplify, simplify*. I only want to present strategies that:

- Give you the biggest ROI
- In the shortest time
- For the least money and hassle

Right now Facebook fits the bill as the best because it's still where most of your customers are. According to a report released by the Pew Research Center, 68% of Americans are on Facebook. This dwarfs the number on Twitter (21%), Instagram (28%), Pinterest (26%), and LinkedIn (25%).

This doesn't make the other sites bad. You can make money using these other platforms, and if you have the time and resources to design and run effective marketing campaigns on multiple social media platforms, go for it. But most dealers barely have the time to effectively implement *one* social media platform, let alone many. So, the question becomes this: out of all the social media platforms available, which *one* is most effective?

When it comes to which platform can do the best job, sending you the most customers—which one actually puts *enough money* in your pocket to make it worth doing—Facebook is still the most effective. Done correctly it can produce a steady stream of high-margin customers for your business.

Watch Out!

Profile vs. Page: not knowing the difference can cause big trouble

Your FB **profile** is your personal site where you post photos of your dog, your vacation, and that five-layer triple-fudge whip-cream-and-chocolate decadence sundae that the waiter just set in front of you.

Your FB **page** is your business site where you promote your dealership.

It's currently against FB guidelines to use your personal profile to promote your business. Doing so can get your profile shut down. If you plan to market your dealership on FB, make sure you set up a business page.

4 deadly FB marketing mistakes
(if you're on FB you're making at least 1 of these)

Most dealers who attempt Facebook marketing make little if any money. This is because they make some key mistakes that hurt their efforts.

Mistake #1: Facebook page is not set up correctly

Many dealers don't set up and optimize their page correctly, and this hurts their efforts. Here are some common set up mistakes:

- Using incomplete information.
- Information and branding is inconsistent with other online listings. Remember, you want consistent information across all platforms.
- No call to action.
- No link to the dealer's main website.
- Weak or non-existent Unique Selling Proposition (USP).

- Setting up their business as a personal profile. This is currently against Facebook's guidelines and can get your profile shut down, as well as any pages associated with it.

Mistake #2: Trying to sell directly on Facebook

Running special offers, or otherwise trying to sell directly on Facebook is not very effective for big ticket items like flooring. People are on social media to be social, not to make high ticket purchases. Your goal with Facebook is to get prospects OFF Facebook and INTO your store or INTO your database, not to try and directly sell flooring.

In figure 2.1 is a flooring special offer posted by a dealer with over 2,000 followers. You'll see that he only got 2 likes. This is very low engagement for this many followers.

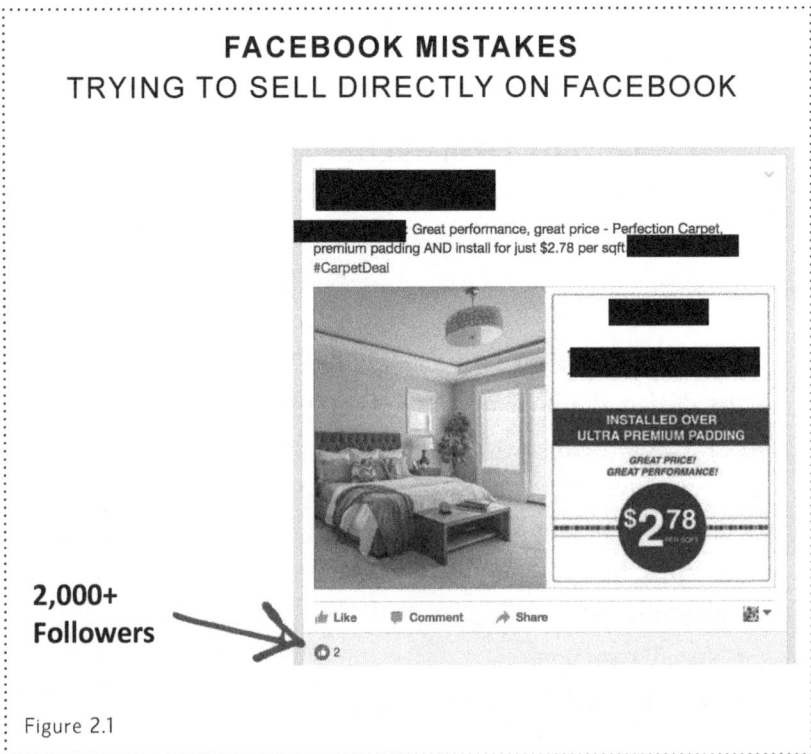

FACEBOOK MISTAKES
TRYING TO SELL DIRECTLY ON FACEBOOK

: Great performance, great price - Perfection Carpet, premium padding AND install for just $2.78 per sqft.
#CarpetDeal

INSTALLED OVER
ULTRA PREMIUM PADDING

GREAT PRICE!
GREAT PERFORMANCE!

$2.78

2,000+
Followers

Like   Comment   Share

2

Figure 2.1

Mistake #3: Photos of sample displays

Photos of sample displays and/or products is also not very effective. In figure 2.2 is a post featuring a sample display. This dealer also has over 2,000 followers, but this post only generated 2 likes.

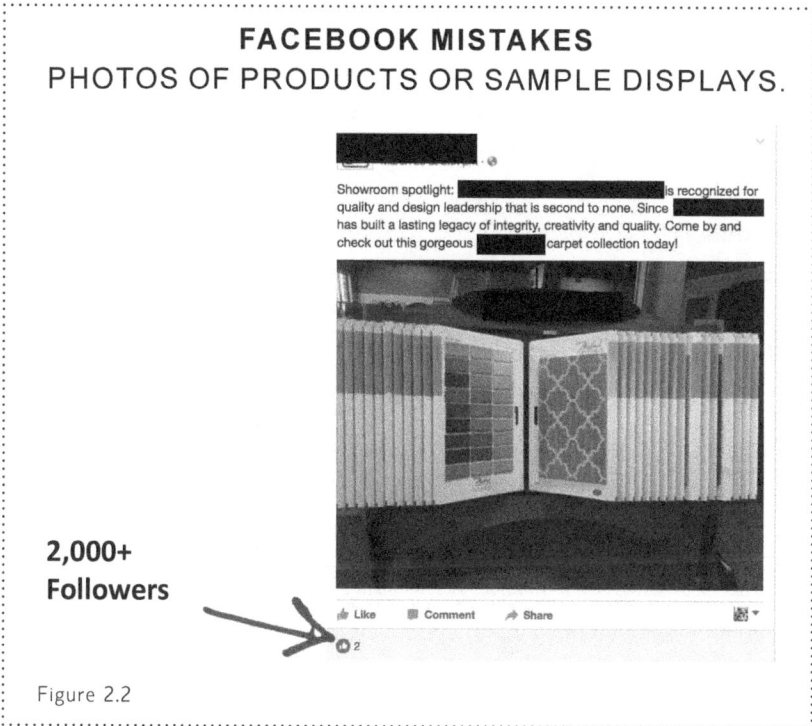

FACEBOOK MISTAKES
PHOTOS OF PRODUCTS OR SAMPLE DISPLAYS.

Showroom spotlight: ███████████████ is recognized for quality and design leadership that is second to none. Since █████ has built a lasting legacy of integrity, creativity and quality. Come by and check out this gorgeous ██████ carpet collection today!

2,000+
Followers

👍 Like   💬 Comment   ➡ Share

Figure 2.2

Mistake #4: Having no FB marketing system

Many dealers simply post photos of products or special offers periodically, with no thought-out plan for systematically generating business from this platform. Simply putting out posts, even regularly, does not mean you have a system. Your posts must fit into an overall plan for generating customers, and each post should do one of three very specific tasks to make that happen. (More about that shortly.)

> **Watch Out!**
>
> ## Never buy Facebook Likes
>
> Having thousands of likes on your FB page makes you look more relevant, and if the likes are from real followers—and you market to them properly—they can translate into big revenue for your business. However, it can be tempting to buy likes, and there are companies all over the internet offering to sell them to you. This is about the worst FB mistake dealers make. If you have 10,000 likes from fake followers not interested in your product, then they are going to have low engagement. This hurts the visibility of your posts, and your real followers won't see them. Fake followers are also not going to buy your product. Fixing all the problems caused by buying likes is very difficult.
>
> BOTTOM LINE: don't buy likes. And if you hire a company to help you with FB, make sure they're not buying likes on your behalf. My company never, ever buys likes for dealers. We generate real likes through effective marketing, and so should you.

3-Step System to Generate Customers on Facebook

There is only one reason to do Facebook marketing: *to get customers to buy from you.* Period. (Actually, this applies to any marketing you're doing, either online or offline.)

You're not on Facebook to...

- Build your brand
- Get your name "out there"
- Create engagement (unless it's part of a comprehensive strategy to drive customers to buy from you)

You're there to get customers.

Figure 2.3 illustrates the simple, 3-step system my team and I use to generate customers for dealers using FB.

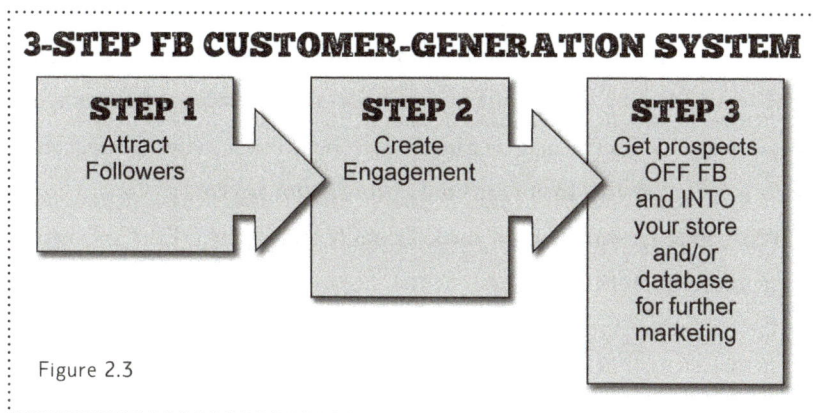

3-STEP FB CUSTOMER-GENERATION SYSTEM

STEP 1
Attract
Followers

STEP 2
Create
Engagement

STEP 3
Get prospects
OFF FB
and INTO
your store
and/or
database
for further
marketing

Figure 2.3

In fact, every single post should do one or more of these three steps. When doing FB marketing for dealers, we use different kinds of posts, and each one does one or more of these steps. Here are some examples:

- Sales-Generation Contest: offering an incentive to engage with that series of posts.
- List-Building Contest: using FB ads to expose your page to new people, and get them to become followers.
- Newsletter subscription posts.
- Customer recognition: Customer of the month.
- Customer recognition: Congratulate Suzy Smith on her new flooring!
- Highlight of your Referral program.
- Team member recognition.
- Trusted Advisor posts (design tips, repair tips, etc.).
- Inspirational posts.
- Community events.
- Holiday posts
  (contests, customer recognition, community events).

Always work within Facebook's guidelines, and use the nature and style of the FB platform to your advantage. You see, posting on Facebook is very different than posting on Instagram or Twitter, even though they're all social media platforms. Facebook style is social, light-hearted, very visual but with a good mix of written text as well. (By contrast, Twitter's focus is mostly text 'headlines,' while Instagram's focus is images with less emphasis on written text.)

With that in mind, let's look at each step of the FB Customer-Generation system.

Step 1: Attract followers

Followers are the "herd" of people who like your page. Gathering followers (or likes) gives you the opportunity to engage with them and market to them. If you don't have many followers, then your first step is to grow your herd. You must be careful with this step, though. The only thing more important than growing your herd is making sure you're growing the *right* herd. If you attract a lot of followers who aren't really interested in flooring, you could be killing the visibility of your page with each new like. This is because if you have a large herd of followers who don't engage with your posts, Facebook's algorithms will penalize your posts by making them visible to fewer people. You want to attract followers who will continue to be interested in what you post throughout your relationship with them. In other words followers who are engaged. If you attract followers who ultimately aren't interested in what you have to offer, you're wasting your time—and your hard-earned money.

There are multiple ways to attract followers including contests, ads, links from your website and email signature, printed and verbal requests. We'll go over several of these options in the following pages.

Step 2: Create engagement

Engagement means that after you post something, people like the post, share it, or comment on it.

Remember that people on FB are there to be social and to be entertained. The most engaging posts are easily-consumed little snacks, like potato chips for the brain. They should be fun and compel interaction with your page and your company.

The posts that typically get the *least* engagement are text-heavy posts. If all you're doing is writing text-heavy messages on Facebook, don't count on a lot of engagement. Posts with eye-catching images and video containing useful information are the ones that get the most attention. Posts that highlight existing followers of the page tend to get even more engagement. We use dozens of different kinds of posts to create engagement for dealers.

You can't deposit "Engagements"

Some social media trainers focus almost solely on how to get engagement, which can lead dealers to believe that this is the ultimate goal of social media marketing. This is total B.S.

The ultimate goal of any marketing, including social media, is this: *to put money in your bank account.* Period. Bankers won't let you deposit "engagement" into your account, only cash. They're picky that way.

Engagement is very important, but if you stop there, your marketing strategy is incomplete. You must turn engagement into sales. If you don't, you're wasting your time.

Step 3: Get prospects OFF Facebook and INTO your store and/or database for further marketing

Your ultimate goal with Facebook is to get them off of that platform and either 1) into your store, or 2) into your own database.

Get prospects into your store

The reason for this is obvious: so you can sell 'em flooring! The only products that tend to sell well on Facebook are low-end, impulse items like costume jewelry and screen print t-shirts. In terms of selling, think of Facebook as a large mall. You don't usually see high-ticket items like flooring being sold in malls where people tend to browse for impulse buys. If you want to make money with Facebook, you've got to get them *off* Facebook.

Get prospects into your own database

You might be wondering why you want to move prospects from FB into your own company database. There are several reasons, but the most important is this: *so you can market to them independently of Facebook.*

You see, you have complete control over your own database and how you communicate with your contacts. Not so with Facebook. Their rules and guidelines change, and what was allowed yesterday may not be allowed tomorrow.

Let's say you attract 10,000 Facebook followers (likes), and let's say that by using the strategies in this book you get 2,000 of them to give you their email address. You can now market to those 2,000 contacts in any way you wish. It doesn't matter what Facebook does. They could even shut your page down, and it wouldn't hurt you because those 2,000 contacts are in a database you own.

Use Facebook as a list-building machine

Remember that people are on FB to have fun, to eat potato chips for their brain. That's why pitches to buy flooring or promos for special offers aren't very effective when they're done as FB posts. Which is why you want to capture their contact information: so you can market to them *outside* of FB. This opens up a whole new, highly effective marketing opportunity to directly drive sales.

By getting contacts into your own database, you're using Facebook as a giant list-building machine. This is a powerful, proven marketing strategy that's commonly used by savvy marketers outside of the flooring industry, but rarely within our industry. It's something that most dealers—including your competitors—simply never figure out. By doing this you give yourself a massive marketing advantage.

So how do you get FB followers to give you their contact info? One effective method is to offer your followers a free gift in exchange for their email address. A great gift to give away is a free report containing information that 1) is related to what you sell, and 2) they desperately want—information so compelling and valuable that they will give you their email address in exchange for it. In the next chapter I outline how this is done, and how you can easily apply this strategy on FB.

Let's dive deeper into the most effective ways to put a Customer Generation System into place on Facebook.

Contests

Facebookers love contests, quizzes, and other forms of entertainment on Facebook. Pick the right prize and format and your contest can get good engagement. Running contests on a regular basis as part of your overall Facebook marketing system ensures you have an ever-growing, consistently engaged follower base.

You can use contests to achieve all three of our main goals on Facebook:

1. Grow your "herd" of followers

Because your goal with this contest is to get more people to 'like' your page, this type of contest must be run through a Facebook Ad. This is the only way to allow those who haven't yet liked your page to see your contest post, so there will be a monetary investment.

With this type of contest, you'll need to keep track of all new people who 'like' your page during the timeframe of your contest. Everyone who likes your page gets entered into your contest, you'll choose your winner from this list.

2. Increase engagement on your page

On Facebook, engagement is important, and engagement means any type of reaction to one of your posts (likes, comments or shares). It doesn't matter how many followers you have if they never see your content, and your followers won't see your content if you don't have an engaged follower base. An engagement contest encourages your list to 'engage' with your posts in exchange for a chance to win a prize.

46

You can run an engagement contest with a simple series of posts, the first one listing clearly what the prize is, the time frame for the contest, and all rules. You may add a second or third post to promote your contest, then wrap it up with a post announcing the winner.

3. Get your followers off of Facebook

Whether you run a list-building contest or an engagement contest, the final goal is to get the winner into your store or into your database. Getting them into your store is easily achieved by offering a prize they must come to pick up. Your contest rules should clearly state what the winner must do to collect their prize – in this case visiting your store to pick up the prize. It's also possible to get non-winners into your store by giving them a special offer or a "second place" prize. (If you run a mobile showroom, they should have to call to get their prize. Schedule an appointment to drop it off at their house. Get a photo while you're there. This is the way to handle any prize or give-away if you don't have a brick-and-mortar location.)

4 Steps to a Successful Contest on Facebook
1. Choose a prize

    a. Prizes should be related to your company such as an area rug, a cleaning kit, etc. No iPads! Offering an iPad (or other product not related to flooring) as a prize may generate engagement and followers, but these followers aren't necessarily interested in flooring. They just want the iPad. *These are not valuable followers*. This is not much different than buying likes. You'll wind up with a bunch of followers who won't engage with most of your posts, which hurts your visibility. Not good.

2. **Decide on your contest rules**

   a. Contests should be very easy to enter. For example, "Like or comment on this post for a chance to win a new area rug." Keep it simple.

   b. As of the writing of this book, it's against Facebook's guidelines to ask entrants to share your contest on their profiles. (See Facebook's Promotions Guidelines for current rules.)

3. **Create your post**

   a. Photos or videos are always best—FB loves eye-catching content.

   b. Be very clear that you're running a contest. Your post should clearly outline the prize, dates of the contest, rules etc.

3. **Announce the winner**

   a. Ask for their email address (this helps build your email list) so you can send them instruction on how to collect their prize. IMPORTANT: They should have to come into your store to collect their prize. This will allow you to snap a selfie with the happy winner and give you more Facebook content.

Figure 2.4 is a post from an engagement contest hosted by Max, a dealer from Texas. This single post generated over 250 likes, and over 250 shares. And this was only one post out of several that were pushed out for this contest, each one getting similar results.

When I interviewed Max, he had already generated over $5,000 in revenue from this contest, and it was still driving walk-in traffic. At this time he was generating 6% of his total sales volume from FB.

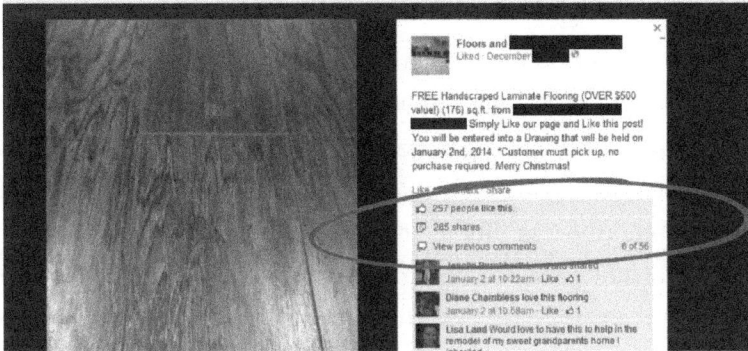

Figure 2.4

More on successful posts

In between running successful contests, it's important to keep Facebook working for you. Keep your followers entertained and engaged with strategically planned posts.

1. Customer recognition (generates engagement)

People love to be recognized! If you post a photo of your customers standing on their beautiful new floors and ask your followers to congratulate them, you're going to get engagement. Better still, get your happy customers to share that post on their FB profiles and you'll get exposed to *their* list of friends. Who wouldn't want to like or leave a comment on a post featuring their friend, and letting them know how great their new floors look? This kind of post can serve a dual purpose: to create engagement *and* to attract new followers. Now you've got potential customers seeing their friends on FB showing off the beautiful new floors you installed. Think about the impact that has on your reputation and trustworthiness. These posts function as social proof; they create differentiation and further position your store as the obvious choice.

2. Be a giver of gifts (gets followers off FB and into your store)

Customers love being recognized and receiving gifts! Dealers we work with select a 'Facebook Follower of the Month' to receive a surprise gift. This gift could be anything from a gift certificate to a local coffee shop, movie tickets or a carpet or hard-surface spotting/cleaning kit. Create a post listing the name of the follower and instructions to come pick up their gift in your store before a deadline (the deadline is important), or to call you if you run a mobile showroom. Using a prize unrelated to flooring is okay in this case because you're rewarding people who are already followers, not trying to attract new ones.

3. Offer a free informational download (achieves getting a follower into your database)

It's important that you offer information that's so valuable and interesting that your follower is willing to give her email address in exchange for your free offer. In the next chapter I outline a strategy to doing this, and how you can apply it to your Facebook marketing.

STRATEGY #3:

....

THE ULTIMATE ONLINE CUSTOMER-CAPTURE SYSTEM

FLOOR DEALER: My website has a bunch of beautiful, professional photos of products rotating across the top of the home page. It has our entire product catalogue. And it has a form so people can schedule an estimate right online! The whole thing is very professional looking.

JIM: Does it answer the unspoken question on each of your prospects' minds?

FLOOR DEALER: What's that?

JIM: "Why should I buy from you instead of your competitor down the street who's cheaper than you?"

FLOOR DEALER: Hmmmm....

How your customers are buying flooring in the New Millennium

Synchrony Financial did a Major Purchase study which focused on the path-to-purchase consumers take when they buy big ticket items. (Big ticket defined as $500 or more.) 85% of consumers begin their path-to-purchase online. 70% then visit a brick-and-mortar store. 82% make their purchase in the store. According to GE Financial, this entire process takes a whopping 79 days on average. Figure 3.1 illustrates the results of both studies.

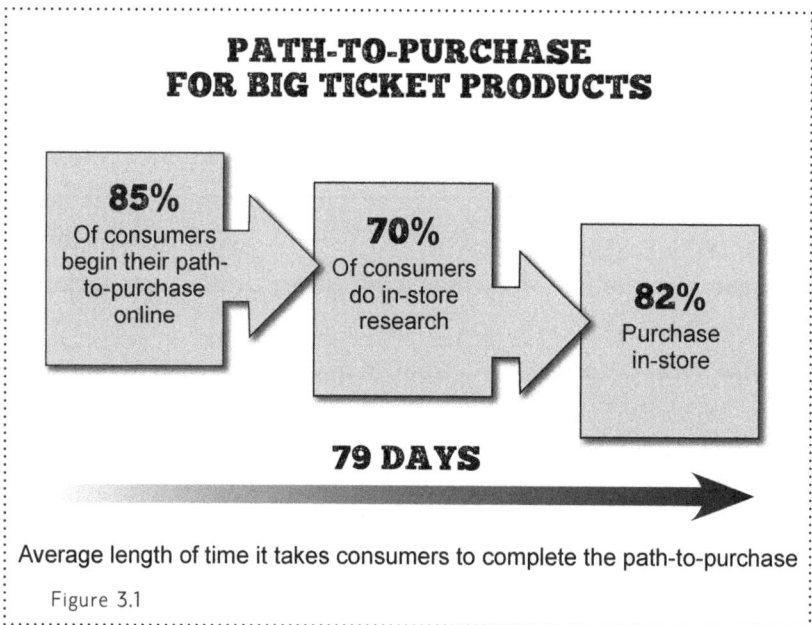

PATH-TO-PURCHASE FOR BIG TICKET PRODUCTS

85% Of consumers begin their path-to-purchase online

70% Of consumers do in-store research

82% Purchase in-store

79 DAYS

Average length of time it takes consumers to complete the path-to-purchase

Figure 3.1

Therefore, the goal of your website is to do four things:
1. **Create differentiation** to make your dealership the overwhelmingly obvious, to the point where people want to visit your store and ONLY your store (or phone you if you run a mobile showroom)
2. **Have a strong call to action** which moves prospects along the 79-day path-to-purchase towards *you,* and away from competitors

3. **Capture prospects' contact information** so you can…

4. **Do follow up marketing** in order to stay in front of prospects throughout the 79-day path-to-purchase

Let's take a look at why most floor dealer websites fail to do any of these things:

Why your website is sending customers flocking to the box stores

There are four problems with most dealers' websites that cause them to lose sales to box stores, online dealers and other competitors.

Problem #1: Failure to create differentiation

Virtually all flooring websites say the same thing. How many websites have you seen that follow this formula:

1. The business name at the top,

2. Photos of products (sometimes with teaser prices or a discount offer), and

3. Contact information?

It's about all you see. I call these "Name, Rank and Serial Number" websites. (Does your website follow this formula?) Yes, flooring websites vary in color and layout. Most have an "about us" section and a product catalogue. A lot of them have a "design your room" widget. But almost everybody has these things, and that's the problem. Superficially these sites vary, but they are all *saying* the same thing. And this creates no differentiation from your competitors. And when there's no differentiation, how do your customers make a buying decision?

On price!

Dealers who build large, successful businesses, and command margins of 45%- 50% or more don't do it by copying all the other dealers. They do it by creating differentiation.

Does your website answer the unspoken question on every prospective customer's mind?

Every one of your prospective customers who is searching online has one burning question on their mind: *Why should I buy from you instead of your competitors?*

They are desperate for an answer to this question.

The bad news is that if you're using a "traditional" name, rank and serial number website, then you are not answering that question. You're not creating differentiation from your competitors, which forces your customers to make their choice based on price.

Or, even worse, you lose them to a competitor without ever getting a shot at their business. They bypassed you completely because as far as they could tell from your website, you're no different than all the other flooring stores. (This is called an online customer leak.)

Yes, there are dealers using name, rank and serial number sites who are able to command premium prices. However, they are doing this *in spite of* their copy-cat website, not because of it. They almost certainly have compensating factors in place—such as skilled sales people—that help make up for the fact that their website does not answer the unspoken question. How many more sales could they close if their website answered the unspoken question before prospects ever set foot in their store? How much easier would their sales team's job be?

Also, by not setting up their website to answer the unspoken question, they are still losing prospects to the competition without realizing it, because they have an online customer leak. Not good.

Will they choose you during their path-to-purchase?

If you fail to create differentiation, then when a prospect reaches the end of the 79-day path-to-purchase (Fig. 3.1), you'll lose them to a dealership that does a better job of creating differentiation. Or they'll go with a name they feel familiar and comfortable with like Home Depot, Lowes, Empire, etc.

Problem #2: A weak or non-existent call to action

Most flooring websites are basically electronic brochures. Like a brochure, they give product and business information. But rarely do they have a strong call to action. Your website should compel visitors to take specific action that propels them down the path-to-purchase *towards* you and *away* from competitors.

A lot of websites have a "Schedule a free estimate" form as their call to action. The problem is that when a prospect is clicking around online, she's in "shopping" mode, not "buying" mode. Offering an estimate at this point is too soon in most cases. It's like a man meeting an attractive woman and immediately saying, "Hi, my name's Bill. Will you marry me?" It's too soon.

Problem #3: Failure to capture your visitor's contact info

You've invested money into having your website built. You're paying hosting fees, and maintenance fees. You may have paid an SEO company to improve your rankings so people can find you. You may have invested large sums into pay-per-click ads to drive people to your site. Yet after investing all this money to drive prospects to your site, most of them simply poke around for a minute and then vanish forever. You're only giving yourself one shot at this prospect's business, and that's it! Once they leave your site...BOOM...you're done. Only a fraction of website visitors ever set foot in your store, so most of the money you invested driving them to your site is wasted. But if you capture their contact information you have the opportunity to stay in front of them throughout the 79-day path-to-purchase.

Problem #4: Failure to do follow up marketing

The goal with follow up marketing is to transform a single website visit into unlimited opportunities stay in front of prospects and win their business.

Because most flooring websites do a poor job of capturing visitors' contact info, there is rarely an opportunity for follow up marketing. As I said earlier, some sites have a "request a free estimate" form. However, when that rare prospect fills out a "free estimate" form, this generally results in a phone call from the dealer, nothing more. This follow up isn't bad, it's just incomplete. A dealer who does this is only getting a small fraction of the value of that lead. It is possible to "touch" that prospect many more times with valuable, informative, welcome, entertaining marketing, and stay in front of them during the 79-day path-to-purchase.

What if there was a single solution to losing customers online?

There are hundreds of website strategies for creating differentiation, building an effective call to action, capturing contact information, and doing follow up marketing. But remember: we want to simplify, simplify, simplify. So let's look at a single solution which solves all these problems.

Kick the boxes where it hurts with the ultimate online customer-capture system

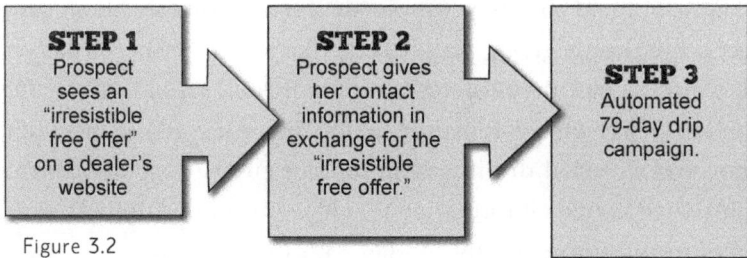

THE ULTIMATE ONLINE CUSTOMER-CAPTURE SYSTEM

STEP 1 Prospect sees an "irresistible free offer" on a dealer's website

STEP 2 Prospect gives her contact information in exchange for the "irresistible free offer."

STEP 3 Automated 79-day drip campaign.

Figure 3.2

Figure 3.2 lays out the 3-step lead capture and follow up system that we implement for floor dealers. Let's break down each step.

Step 1: Prospect sees an "irresistible free offer"

By "irresistible," I mean an offer so compelling that a total stranger is willing to give you her contact information in order to get her hands on what you're giving away. In creating this kind of offer it's important to understand the mindset of someone shopping for flooring. She is excited about the prospect of getting new floors to make her home more beautiful. She is about to invest thousands of dollars, so she doesn't want to make a mistake by purchasing the wrong flooring and having to live with a decision she'll regret. And she doesn't want to get stuck working with a dishonest or incompetent dealer, or wind up with a shoddy installation. Her excitement is combined with some nervousness, which is part of the reason the path-to-purchase averages 79 days. She's researching online looking for answers—for guidance.

What if you're the one to offer her this guidance? And what if you were able to quickly position yourself as a highly competent Trusted Advisor before she even set foot in your store? It's possible, and here's how:

Imagine a consumer who's just beginning the 79-day path-to-purchase. She sees one name-rank-and-serial-number website after another, and they aren't helping her make a decision on which dealer to choose, because every site is saying essentially the same thing. None of them are answering her unspoken question: *why should I buy from you instead of your competitors?*

Then she visits your flooring site, and instantly it's obvious that something is different. She sees a video or ad which makes an irresistible offer. In the ad or video she learns that the thousands of choices of flooring can make the purchase process confusing and overwhelming. And that by downloading your free *Consumer's Guide To Floor Covering*™ she can get the information she needs to find an honest, trustworthy dealer, and find the perfect floors. The ad or video also explains that by downloading the guide she will learn:

- "How to avoid predatory dealers"
- "6 mistakes to avoid when choosing a flooring store"
- "5 questions to ask a dealer before you buy anything"

This strategy, including the *Consumer's Guide To Floor Covering*™, is what we set up for dealers we work with. It's a compelling offer that makes prospects eager to provide their contact information. Does everyone share their information? Of course not, but a percentage do. These are highly valuable, hot prospects, worth their weight in gold. Here's why:

Most advertising (both online and offline) is massively wasteful because you're spending time, energy and money to reach thousands of people who aren't in the market for flooring. What if you could identify the people in your market who are looking to buy flooring right away? Who *right now* are on the 79-day path-to-purchase?

This is exactly what the above strategy allows you to do. Now you can zero in on these people with your follow up marketing, and stay in front of them throughout the 79 days.

Step 2: Prospect gives her contact information in exchange for the "irresistible free offer"

You need to collect three pieces of information: name, email address and phone number. Some will argue that by asking for their phone number, you'll cut down on response. You might, but here's why a lower response rate actually helps you in this case:

Depending on the size of your market there are tens or hundreds-of-thousands of home owners who can afford your products. However, only a small percentage need your product in any given month. Most advertising is terribly wasteful because it goes out to all these thousands upon thousands of people, most of whom don't need flooring.

That's why good marketing is a process of sifting, sorting and screening out the thousands of non-customers to find the hot prospects who are predisposed to buy from you right away. It's like panning for gold. You want to filter out all the dirt and debris so you're left with only the gold nuggets.

If a prospect is willing to give you her name, email AND phone number, she has raised her hand and identified herself as a hot prospect who is *very* interested in buying flooring. She is a gold nugget! You can now focus more intense marketing efforts on her.

After she gives you her contact info (opts in), she downloads the irresistible free offer, in this example, the *Consumer's Guide To Floor Covering*™. I've engineered this guide so it not only serves as the "bait" to obtain the contact information of hot prospects, but it's written in such a way that it does several other important jobs as well:

- It positions the dealer as a Trusted Advisor, like a family doctor.
- It can shorten the path-to-purchase. If the prospect feels like she has found someone she can trust, she may stop "shopping around" immediately and simply buy from you.
- It creates differentiation from the competition. The guide looks and sounds different than any traditional advertising the prospect has seen.
- It makes the dealer the obvious choice.
- It stacks the deck in favor of the dealer, giving them an "unfair" advantage over competitors. For example, one section includes "5 Questions to Ask A Dealer Before You Buy." These questions strongly favor the dealer giving away the guide.
- It helps the dealer command premium prices.

Step 3: Automated 79-day drip campaign

Now that you've collected your prospect's contact information, and she has identified herself as someone very interested in buying flooring, you can subscribe her to more intensive marketing efforts.

One goal in the first 30 days after opting in is to shorten the 79-day path-to-purchase. By using communication that creates differentiation and positions you and your team as Trusted Advisors, you can give your prospects such a high level of comfort, that she may decide that she's found the right dealer, and that further "shopping around" is unnecessary, even unwise. With this in mind, the first 30 days after opting in should consist of the most intensive sales and marketing efforts.

Days 1-30

Every 2 to 3 days your prospect should get an email from you. Every email should follow the 90/10 formula: 90% great content, and only 10% consisting of an invitation to purchase. Let's break it down:

90% great content

This means content she will find valuable, informative, welcome, and entertaining. Each email should be so compelling that she's eager to read it and even forward it to her friends. Emails should continue the job that the *Consumer's Guide* began by doing the following jobs:

- Position you as a Trusted Advisor, like a family doctor
- Shorten the 79-day path-to-purchase by giving her such a high level of comfort that she is likely to stop "shopping around" and settle on doing business with you rather than one of your competitors
- Create differentiation
- Make you the obvious choice
- Stack the deck in your favor, giving you an "unfair" advantage over competitors.
- Help you command premium prices

60

10% invitation to buy

Up to 10% of the message can consist of a special offer or invitation to purchase. You should include a deadline for the offer, and a very clear, simple call to action: to phone you or visit your showroom.

Many dealers doing email marketing send out messages that are 100% advertisements. Doing this is likely to turn your prospect off and cause her to opt out of receiving emails.

Your "unfair" advantage over competitors

By convincing a prospect to opt in for your free offer, you have bought yourself the opportunity to send her your first email. If that first email contains valuable information she wants, needs and enjoys, then she won't opt out. Congratulations! You've just bought yourself the opportunity to send her a *second* email. And so on. In this way, you can stay in front of prospects (and past customers) indefinitely, which gives you unlimited opportunities to sell to them and generate referrals from them. That's extremely powerful, and something none of your competitors likely understand.

Talk about an unfair advantage! While the box stores and other competitors are spamming their lists with a barrage of advertisements (and as a result causing many of their contacts to opt out), you are building long-lasting, deep connections with your list. You are rounding up a herd of people who know you, like you, and trust you; who are predisposed to buy from you again and again. Who send you referrals. This is something the vast majority of dealers will never, ever understand. By making this shift in your marketing efforts you give yourself a de-facto unfair advantage over every other competitor in your market. This shift is largely responsible for the incredible success dealers have had using the systems I teach. (See the Appendix for dealer case studies.)

Outbound phone call

Within a day or two of opting in for your free offer, your prospect should get a phone call from a member of your sales team. There is one goal, and one goal only for this call: to schedule an appointment, either in your showroom or the prospect's home. Begin the conversation by asking if she received the *Consumer's Guide,* and if she has, any questions. The conversation should then segue into scheduling an appointment.

Remember: people who opt in for your free offer have raised their hands and indicated that they are interested in buying flooring, that *right now* they are on the path-to-purchase. By implementing this strategy you are creating a steady stream of hot leads for your sales team.

Days 31-79

If the prospect fails to schedule an appointment or visit your showroom in the first 30 days of intensive marketing, this doesn't mean they aren't interested. It likely means that they are still deciding which dealer to use. Therefore, it's critically important to stay in front of them regularly throughout the remainder of the 79-day path-to-purchase. So for days 31-79 send an email every 5-7 days, less frequently than during the first 30 days. Your messages should follow the same 90/10 formula. Your goals are still the same—to position you and your team as Trusted Advisors, to create differentiation, to get the prospect to choose you instead of your competitors, etc.

One or two more outbound phone calls during this time are also important. They show that you care, that you are different, and that you really value their business. All positives. Remember: the ultimate goal for these calls is to schedule an appointment.

How to use the Ultimate Lead Capture strategy on Facebook

In the last chapter I explained the importance of getting people off FB and into your own database. The "Ultimate Lead Capture" strategy is an effective, proven way to do this.

First, create a post offering the free report, explaining how your prospect will benefit by getting a copy. This is an important step because, as stated above, you've got to overcome her reluctance to give you her email address. Once a prospect requests the report offered on your post, subscribe her to the 79-day follow up campaign.

CASE STUDY

Secret weapon makes customers see this dealer as the obvious choice

Sam Quandahl is the owner of Floor Coverings of Winona in Minnesota. He has made customer education a part of his sales process by using the *Consumer's Guide To Floor Covering*™ which I discussed in this chapter.

His sales team is excited about this tool. One day one of them pulled him aside and told him that some "skeptical shoppers" came into the store to buy flooring. When they left—without buying—she gave them the *Consumer's Guide*. A few days later the couple came back and told her that they had shopped at several other stores, but were going to buy from Floor Coverings of Winona. This in spite of the fact that Sam's dealership is more expensive than most of his competitors. They told her that a big part of their decision was because of the impression the *Consumer's Guide* had made on them.

The salesperson asked these customers what she could do to exceed their expectations. Their reply: "You already have!" They then immediately scheduled an appointment to have their house measured. No hesitation. No needing to "think about it." When Sam was through measuring, they demanded that he take a check, even though they hadn't decided on the final color.

Another customer commented to Sam: "As we were reading through the *Consumer's Guide*, it really made us feel that you want to know what we need and what will really help us. It made it very personable." She also bought from Sam rather than his lower-priced competitors.

How to implement all 3 digital strategies in your business

Implementation checklist

Next is a checklist covering each of the strategies in this book, and how to implement them into your flooring business.

✓ Setting up your bullet-proof, 5-Star Review System

☑ Search the web for all existing reviews on all major review sites and as many smaller review sites local to your area as you can find. A partial list includes Google My Business, Yelp, Houzz, Home Advisor, Angie's List, and Facebook.

☑ Confirm that your account or profile is officially claimed and fully set up on every review site. Important: just seeing reviews on a site doesn't mean you've officially set up your account on that site. People can leave reviews on a site you haven't claimed.

- Each review site has a slightly different platform, user interface and format, so you'll want to read their guidelines on how each works and what their standards are.

☑ Make sure your contact information is exactly the same on every online platform. This includes all review sites, such as Google My Business, as well as social media platforms, and your business website.

☐ Set up your review filter. This minimizes negative reviews, and gives you the chance to address customer complaints before they are made public on the major review sites. A review filter works like this:

- Ask customers to rate your business from 1 to 5 stars. This rating should take place on a website you control, NOT on the review sites.

- If a customer gives you 3 stars or less, your system should immediately notify you via email, so you can address the problem with your customer. Many of these can be turned into 4 or 5-star reviews simply by addressing your customer's complaint.

- • If a customer gives you a 4 or 5-star rating, your system should provide a link to one of the review sites and ask them to write a review.

❑ Record links to all review sites that you have claimed, so you can monitor the sites on a regular basis, and so you can make changes to your profile if needed.

❑ Monitor each and every review site weekly, so you can respond to any negative reviews right away. Your review filter will stop most negative reviews from reaching the review sites, but not all of them. This makes monitoring all your review sites on a weekly basis very important.

- • We've automated this step for our dealers. They get a list of all reviews from all major review sites weekly, and instant notification of negative reviews that occur in the review filter.

❑ Keep reviews coming in on a regular basis, and spread over various review sites. Consumers are wary of businesses that don't have recent reviews, or even worse, have no reviews on their preferred review source. The Google-bots don't like a flood of reviews coming in at once because it's an indicator of fraud. A consistent drip of reviews is much better than dozens hitting the internet all at once.

❑ Amplify positive ratings. When someone gives you a 4 or 5-star rating in your review filter, ask them to leave a review on Google My Business, Yelp, Angie's List, or Facebook. Stream positive reviews on your business website.

❑ *Make sure each and every customer knows you want them to write a review.* Provide your sales people with scripts for asking for reviews, as well as printed requests. Also send email reminders to your customers after the installation is complete.

Setting up your Facebook Customer-Generation System

In order to generate customers on FB, you need to get your followers *off* of Facebook and *into* your own database or *into* your store. Do the following with this in mind:

❑ BEFORE SETTING UP YOUR PAGE. Branding is critical for your Facebook page. You want every visitor to your Facebook page to have no doubt about who you are. To achieve this, you should have the same look, feel and 'voice' across all your online platforms. The very first thing people see when they visit your page is your cover photo and 'profile' picture. Let's talk about those 2 important items first.

  • Your Cover photo should closely match the colors and style of your website. Smart Facebookers use the 'header' or top images on their websites as a starting point for their cover photo.

  • Your profile picture (called a 'Profile picture' even on FB Pages) should follow some very basic guidelines to be most effective:

    a. Images are better than words—this is the picture that shows up every time you post or comment on a post, and it's TINY.

    b. Using a picture of the store owner is best. This helps build recognition and puts a face to all the things you're going to be posting.

    c. DON'T use text-heavy pictures. Since these images are tiny, the text will be difficult or impossible to read, and this will only frustrate your followers.

❑ Set up your page as a *local business or place*—this tells Facebook to always make your address available, along with a map of your local area so your followers can find your store easily.

  • This will also allow you to add details about things like parking and hours of operation.

❑ Make sure the contact information listed on your page exactly matches the contact information listed in all of your other online profiles, business website, etc.

❑ Use each part of your Facebook 'About' section to your advantage, regardless of what Facebook suggests you put there. You can have different 'parts' of the About section. Facebook changes these options frequently, so regardless of what you list, monitor your page and make sure all the information you put there stays there, and in an attractive format. Here are some tips for maximizing the effectiveness of your Page's 'About' section:

- Use every opportunity to include a link to your website. Every part of your 'About section' should have a link to a page on your site (i.e. 'See what our happy customers are saying about Jimbo's Floors: www.Jimbosfloors.com/testimonials.)

- Use one of the parts of the 'About section' to list all the advantages of working with your store.

- Use another one of the parts of the 'about' section to highlight your great guarantees & warrantees, and any other unique selling propositions. Link back to the page on your website with that information, too.

- Add a link to your website that allows the visitor to schedule an appointment.

- In other words, use the 'About section' to answer the unspoken question on every prospect's mind: *why should I do business with you instead of your competitors?*

❑ Consider whether or not you'll be able to check your page frequently for private messages. If you don't think you'll be able to get back to private messages fairly quickly (within one day at the very longest), you may consider turning this feature off. If you turn off private messages, be sure to list your email address and phone number. Turning off messages doesn't hinder your followers' ability to communicate with you if done correctly.

❑ Consider the privacy/editing settings on your page, this will vary depending on your anticipated follower base. Facebook currently allows you to set various profanity filters, age limitations, ability for your followers to post to your page – or not, ability for your followers to tag people in your posts – or not. I would suggest thinking about your local community and the likelihood of inappropriate posts/comments on your page, as well as your ability to monitor these contributions when making the decisions about how much to allow on your page.

❑ Post on a regular basis. We post 3 times per week for our dealers. This does not include positive reviews that are automatically pushed out as posts.

- Posts should do one of three jobs: 1) Attract new followers, 2) Generate engagement, 3) Move prospects *off* of FB and *into* your store and/or database.

- We use many kinds of posts to accomplish these three jobs. (See *Strategy #2: The Facebook Customer Generation System* for a list of different posts, and how to create the most effective posts.)

The ultimate online customer capture system

Remember that your website should accomplish four things:

1. **Create differentiation** to make your dealership the overwhelmingly obvious, to the point where people want to visit your store and ONLY your store (or phone you, if you run a mobile showroom)

2. **Have a strong call to action** which moves prospects along the 79-day path-to-purchase *towards* you, and *away* from competitors

3. **Capture prospects' contact information** so you can…

4. **Do follow up marketing** and stay in front of prospects throughout the 79-day path-to-purchase

Below is the checklist to set up the 3-step system that accomplishes all four things.

Step 1: Prospect sees an irresistible offer

❑ On your website feature an ad or video offering valuable information to prospects, such as a free report.

- Your prospect must consider the information valuable enough that she's willing to give you her name, phone number and email address in exchange for it. We provide our floor dealer customers with a report called the *Consumer's Guide To Floor Covering*™ which accomplishes this.

❑ Your ad or video should promote the benefits of downloading the report. In the *Consumer's Guide To Floor Covering*™ report prospects learn how to avoid predatory floor dealers, six costly misconceptions about flooring, and 5 questions to ask a dealer before buying anything. Everything in the *Consumer's Guide* stacks the deck in favor of the dealer using it. If you create your own report it should do the same thing.

- If you're are using a co-op website, you may or may not be able to post an ad or video. If your co-op website doesn't offer this flexibility, then you'll want to set up a separate landing page with the ad or video and an opt-in form. Promote that landing page in your email signature line, your Facebook posts, and anywhere else you're promoting your business.

Step 2: Prospect gives her contact information
in exchange for the irresistible offer

❑ Set up an opt-in form that captures your prospects name, email and phone number.

- If you're using an ad or text box, have it link to your opt-in form.

- If you're using a video, you can have a button below the video that links to your form.

- If you have limited flexibility on your site, you can have a single button offering your report. Make the button a bold, contrasting color so it immediately catches your prospect's eye.

❑ The opt-in form should subscribe your prospect to an automated drip campaign using autoresponder software

Step #3: Automated 79-day drip campaign

❑ Purchase autoresponder software. Autoresponders automatically drip out email content to your prospects who opt-in for your free offer. Make sure the autoresponder you choose also has the ability to notify you when a prospect opts in.

❑ Connect your opt-in form to the autoresponder software. Most autoresponders provide their own opt-in forms which you can add to a page on your site by simply pasting in a line of HTML code. In this case, connection between the form and the autoresponder is "built in."

❑ Program your autoresponder to notify you immediately when a prospect opts in.

❑ Assign these opt-ins to your sales team.

❑ Create an outbound phone call script for your sales team.

❑ Outbound phone call: takes place within 1-2 days of the prospect opting in. The goal is to schedule an appointment either in your showroom or the prospect's home.

❑ Decide on a special offer for your drip campaign.

❑ Write 20 emails that follow the 90/10 formula. (90% of the copy should be educational, fun, informative, welcome, entertaining information which positions you as a Trusted Advisor. Up to 10% of the copy should be an offer to buy flooring from you.)

❑ Program your autoresponder to drip out the first 10 emails over the first 30 days. (One email every 2-3 days.)

  • The first 10 emails should have a strong call to action and a deadline ending on day 30.

  • The goal is to shorten the 79-day path-to-purchase if possible, and steer them towards *your* store and away from competitors.

❑ Program your autoresponder to drip out the remaining emails over days 31-79. (One email every 5-7 days.)

  • If they don't respond in the first 30 days, this doesn't mean they are not interested. They are likely still deciding which dealer to use. That's why it's critical that you stay in front of them for the entire 79-day path-to-purchase.

What you've discovered so far

• How to create a bullet-proof 5-star review system, and why creating a steady-stream of positive reviews is critical to your success in today's market.

• How to build a Facebook customer-generation system, and how to get prospects *off* FB and *into* your store and/or database.

• How to turn your existing website into the ultimate customer-capture system by 1) creating differentiation, 2) having a strong call to action, and 3) capturing your prospects' contact information so you can 4) do follow up marketing.

I want you to understand this one thing: by implementing these strategies you will *finally* be able to magnetically attract the best customers from online. You can quit selling on price, because you're getting customers who are predisposed to buy from you, and will happily pay more because you've positioned your business as the *obvious choice*, and created complete differentiation from the boxes and other competitors. Your customers will respect you and your sales team as Trusted Advisors, like their family doctor. You can literally turn your business around and make plenty of money. No more worrying about making payroll. You'll be able to afford to hire good people, so you can delegate and not have to work so many hours.

How to transform your business and life for the better

Let me repeat that last sentence because it's important: *by making plenty of money, you'll be able to afford to hire good people so you can delegate and not have to work so many hours.*

This is a very, very big deal because overwork is epidemic in our industry. If you're like most dealers you love your business, but you probably also feel like you work too much—that business is too stressful. Think what it would mean to eliminate the stress and burnout from working 60+ hours per week. You can have your nights and weekends free, and be able to spend time with your spouse and kids. When you're away from work, you won't have to worry about your business because you have a system in place generating an ongoing stream of great customers on autopilot. You'll be able to be fully present with your spouse and kids. You'll be able to enjoy vacations, playing golf or other hobbies, traveling, volunteering, exercising, and not have to worry about your business, because all of this is working 24/7. Your business now works for *you* instead of you working for *it*. You'll start looking forward to Mondays, because business is *fun* again!

In other words, these digital strategies can be your doorway to a whole new life in the flooring business.

How good would it feel to have the business and lifestyle I described above in place? I can tell you first-hand from the many dealers I've helped to achieve their *Ideal Business* and *Ideal Lifestyle* that they feel fantastic, and they'll never go back to being slaves to their stores. (You can read their stories in the Appendix section.)

You now have two choices

Choice #1

Your first option is to take the information you've learned in this book and do it yourself, and if that's what you decide to do, great! However, even though I've dramatically simplified online marketing, and identified the only three strategies you need to focus on, you still may be thinking, *"Wow, this is going to take a lot of time and resources to implement. And once they're implemented I've still got to manage them and stay on top of everything every day. Where am I going to find the time? I wish someone could just do it for me."* If this describes you, then you have a second option...

Choice #2

The second way is the easy way, the fast way. And that's to let my team of floor marketing experts implement and manage the strategies in this book *for you* with my proven *Digital Floor Dealer* system. This way you can reap the rewards without having to do the work, and without having to spend months or years of trial and error.

As a business owner, the highest and best use of your time is building your business, not trying to learn, set up and run a digital marketing system. Especially when you can have experts handle it for you.

How to get the whole "digital enchilada" implemented and managed FOR you

I'd like to invite you to check out how my team and I can fully implement all three digital marketing systems and manage them *for you.* All the details are in the materials shipped to you with this book.

Or, you can visit **DigitalFloorDealer.com**.

I look forward to coming alongside you and helping you to Beat the Boxes Online, and transform your business and life for the better!

To Your Success,

Jim Augustus Armstrong

President, *Flooring Success Systems*

Get started Beating the Boxes Online today!
Check out the information shipped with this book, or visit DigitalFloorDealer.com

APPENDIX

....

FLOOR DEALER CASE STUDIES

I began *Flooring Success Systems* in 2007 to help dealers make a lot more money while working a lot less. To help them transform their business into an *Ideal Business* which funds and facilitates their *Ideal Lifestyle*. By implementing the strategies in this book, you can make a lot more money and sell at higher prices. This empowers you to hire strong team members so you can delegate and work less. Instead of spending 60+ hours per week at your business, you can cut that in half and have time for hobbies, golf, fishing, family, or whatever you like. In other words, these strategies can be the doorway to your whole new life in the flooring business.

On the following pages are comments from just some of dealers I've worked with who have transformed their businesses and lives for the better.

I

How Jerome Raised His Margins From 30% to 50% And Stays Booked Out 6-12 Weeks!

Jerome Nowowiejski from Texas is a member of my program and his story should be an inspiration to any dealer who is working too hard for too little, or who thinks that an *Ideal Business* and *Ideal Lifestyle* are impossible for a floor dealer to achieve.

Jerome made an incredible transition in a short period of time, and he has a better business as well as a better life. Before I met Jerome, he had extremely low margins (below 30% on residential) yet within only three months he began commanding margins between 45% and 50% on *all* his residential flooring.

Jerome has had his own flooring store since 2004. Before he put these new systems in place he says the approach was, "Cat and mouse, scratching, trying to get every job you could." He never left the store, and was "worn out … exhausted."

How's business now? Jerome is normally booked out for 2-3 months! He considers it "slow" when he's only booked out for 2 weeks. Why isn't he worried about telling customers they have to wait maybe three months for an installation? Because Jerome has learned to create total differentiation from competitors. Prospects are completely willing to wait weeks or months for their installation, even if a cheaper-priced competitor can do it that day. Most dealers would be terrified to tell a customer they had to wait three months; it's unthinkable. But that's because they have not implemented the strategies Jerome has. He now has total control over his business and his life. He owns his business, not the other way around.

II

In the meantime, he takes a lot of 3-day weekends and several multi-week vacations every year. While he's gone his business runs like a well-oiled machine because he was able to afford to put a great team in place.

Jerome now owns seven houses (some for rental income) and another on a lake nearby. All but one are paid off, and he owns his store and warehouse free and clear. Before joining *Flooring Success Systems* he only had his own home and one rental property, both with mortgages. By investing the extra profits his business now generates into real estate, Jerome will likely have the option of early retirement if he chooses.

Jerome is proving every day that any floor dealer can build their *Ideal Business* and live their *Ideal Lifestyle*, including you. By implementing the digital strategies in this book, you can explode your revenue by getting more sales and commanding higher prices. You'll not only be making a lot more money, you'll be able to afford to hire the best employees so you can delegate and move some of your work off your overloaded plate. Would you like to take 3-day weekends? Take multiple vacations every year? Eliminate the stress? And while you're gone your store continues to run smoothly? Jerome will be the first to tell you that if he can do it, you can, too. The strategies I've outlined in this book can be your doorway to a fantastic new life in flooring retail.

Jimmy Tells Price Shoppers That He's The Most Expensive ... And Still Gets The Sale!

Jimmy Williams is a dealer from North Carolina and has been in business for over 40 years. He has done an outstanding job creating differentiation and positioning himself as a Trusted Advisor. His prices are higher than virtually all his competitors.

Like most dealers, he occasionally has people try to beat him up on price. But he uses one of my sales strategies to instantly turn the tables on them.

"I had a fellow come into the store, trying to beat me up on price," Jimmy told me. "I decided to use the strategy you talk about in your program. I looked him in the eye and told him that we're the highest priced store in the county, and that I'm sorry, but we probably wouldn't be able to help him. I handed him my card, and as I turned away he said, 'But wait ...'"

He bought. At *Jimmy's* price.

This happened twice within a couple of weeks of my conversation with Jimmy. For most dealers, the thought of telling a prospect that they're the most expensive strikes terror in their hearts. But because Jimmy has positioned himself as totally different than competitors, he is not only able to command premium prices, but look price shoppers in the face and tell them he's the most expensive store in the county. And he lands many of those sales. He also instantly snatches away the price shopper's biggest weapon. If she says he's too expensive, he says, "Yup, we're the most expensive in town. We're probably not the right store for you."

BOOM!

What else is the prospect going to say? She's just fired her biggest gun and the bullet bounced off Jimmy's chest.

And it gets even better. By first telling the prospect that he's the most expensive, and then following it up with "We probably won't be able to help you," Jimmy is subtly letting the prospect know that if she doesn't buy from Jimmy, she's proving that she's a cheapskate. Jimmy has turned the prospect's implied insult that "you're not worth the price you're asking" right back on her. Brilliant!

How would it feel to do the same thing with prospects who try to beat *you* up on price? How would it feel to be able to command premium prices? Empowering? Fun? Exhilarating? Liberating? Yup. I've done this in my businesses, and the feeling is amazing. The online strategies in this book are designed to differentiate you from all the other dealers in your market, and make it easy to command margins of 45% or more. You've just got to implement them. We can help you. Check out the materials shipped with this book, or visit DigitalFloorDealer.com.

Florida Dealer Only Works 4 Days Per week, and His Revenue is Way Up!

Before I met Craig Bendele, he was working 60+ hours per week. "I used to work 'dark to dark,' including weekends," He told me. "The stress was terrible."

Craig is a dealer from Florida who grew up in the business. His family has been in the flooring business since the mid 1950's, and in 1975 they moved to Florida and opened a store. He started out at the age of 12, sweeping the floor and mowing the lawn, moving on to warehouse management and scheduling installers. In 2004 he went into sales, and eventually took over as owner in 2011.

"I focused on the minutiae of the business like selling, closing, getting the measurements right, nylon vs. polyester," Craig said. "I hadn't thought about all the stuff that comes at you as an owner like cash flow, advertising details, or sales people showing up out of the blue."

During his first year as owner, Craig stayed on the sales floor handling sales tasks, as well as bookkeeping and all the other responsibilities. He soon found himself falling further and further behind. "A flooring manager and I used to joke that we worked dark to dark," Craig said. "The hours didn't matter, I never looked at a clock, it was just dark to dark. I worked six or seven days a week, 60-plus hours a week. My margins were low and my stress was high."

That's when Craig saw my column in *Floor Covering News*, and inquired about my program.

Within 12 months Craig was working far fewer hours. "I show up each day at 10:00 a.m., I leave by 5:00, and I take Fridays,

Saturdays and Sundays off," Craig said. He only works four days per week, less than 30 hours weekly. This is something most dealers only dream of.

Craig's revenue and margins are up, and his stress levels are down. Not only is he working less, he's making a lot more money. After joining my program, his revenue went up 50% two years in a row! He is able to afford a great in-store team which allows him to work the hours *he* chooses. He and his wife take vacations, and he's no longer shackled to his store.

Not long after implementing these changes in his business, Craig had lunch with a fellow flooring dealer in his town who was new to the business. "As usual, we placed our cell phones on the table in case we got a call," Craig told me. "Mine didn't ring once, but the other guy's cell never stopped. He talked to his installers twice, the salesperson once, handling all the picky little details himself, interrupted some 10-20 times in the course of two hours. No one at my store needed me. It practically runs itself now. But my friend was totally stressed out. He couldn't even get away from his business for two hours without constant interruptions."

Which dealer do you most resemble right now? Craig, who is able to leave his business for hours, days or weeks at a time and it runs without him? Or his friend who can't even go to lunch without 20 interruptions? If you're more like Craig's friend, there is hope. You can have the lifestyle you've always dreamed of. You can step into the kind of life Craig has, and it begins with implementing the strategies in this book.

The best part? We can implement them for you. Check out the materials shipped with this book, or visit DigitalFloorDealer.com.

DEALER COMMENTS

"I made an extra $90,463 in one month using Jim's strategies."
-DAVID KOCIAN, TX

"I'm working less than 30 hours per week, revenue is up 50%...Business is fun again!"
-EARL SWALM, SK

"I'm now taking weekends off, and my wife and I went to Cabo...our first vacation in years!"
-JAY ROBINSON, VA

"...I've Made Over $250,000 In Extra Income...So Far!"
BRENT B, UT

"We love having Home Depot as our neighbor! We take a lot of business from them!
-MARK BOUQUET, IL
(THAT'S MARK IN THE PHOTO)

"I stopped wasting $15,000 - $20,000 per month on advertising...And My Sales Went Up! Thanks, Jim!"
-TIM R., MN

I've only been a member for three months, but because of Jim's systems I've raised my prices 30%...I'm now getting no less than 50% margins on everything I sell. And I'm even busier than before I raised my prices! Thanks, Jim!"

-GARRY & CINDY, IL

"My revenue has doubled and tripled."

STEVE D'ANGELO, AZ

"Our Revenue Is Up 79.3% Over Last Year! Thanks, Jim!"

-MIKE PHOENIX, CT

"Jim, I just wanted you to know that had I not joined AND PUT IT ON A CREDIT CARD, I would have been a statistic. But with the growth of the retail, and the connection, we have been able to carry somehow these massive jobs. So when I say thank you, I want you to know that I believe you were a Godsend. I wish nothing but the best for you and yours Jim. God bless You my Friend,"

-MARK B., IL

"P.S. I am going to make a prediction that we will do 4 to 5 million this coming year!"

"Costa Rica! Blended drinks on the beach with my Bride of 25 plus years, Carolyn. We had a blast! This was our first vacation in 8 years. Jim, thanks for the motivation to let our store work for us rather than us working for the store."

-DAN GINNATY, MT

DON'T ENVY THESE DEALERS... JOIN THEM!

Check out the information shipped with this book,
or visit **DigitalFloorDealer.com.**

ABOUT THE AUTHOR

Jim's surveys of hundreds of flooring dealers have shown that "traditional" advertising methods are failing most of them. Realizing dealers needed help, in 2007 he founded *Flooring Success Systems,* a program which provides done-for-you marketing services, as well as coaching & training in the areas of sales, marketing, and mindset for total business success. His unconventional, turnkey marketing strategies empower dealers to stop wasting money on "traditional" advertising methods, and totally eliminate selling on cheap-price. Through Jim's trainings, dealers learn to create total differentiation from their competitors, charge premium prices, and explode their profits in any market. Jim also trains dealers how to make more money while working less. Dealers are able to grow their business, while at the same time enjoy a fantastic lifestyle. A recurring theme in Jim's trainings (and the name of his coaching newsletter) is *"Ideal Business, Ideal Lifestyle*™.*"* Many floor dealers have quickly achieved stunning success using his methods.

For information about *Flooring Success Systems* contact
his office at 1-877-887-5791.